MW00779273

The God in You

Complete and Unabridged

©2010 Wilder Publications

All rights reserved. Printed in the United States of America. No part of
this book may be used or reproduced in any manner without written
permission except for brief quotations for review purposes only.

Wilder Publications, Inc.
PO Box 243
Blacksburg, VA 24060-0243

ISBN 10: 1-61720-001-8
ISBN 13: 978-1-61720-001-4
First Edition

10 9 8 7 6 5 4 3 2 1

The God in You

By Robert Collier

Table of Contents

THE GOD IN YOU

The declaration of Independence starts with the preamble that all men are born free and equal. But how many believe that? When one child is born in a Park Avenue home, with doctors and nurses and servants to attend to his slightest want, with tutors and colleges to educate him, with riches and influence to start him in his career, how can he be said to be born equal to the child of the Ghetto, who has difficulty getting enough air to breathe, to say nothing of food to eat, and whose waking hours are so taken up with the struggle for existence that he has no time to acquire much in the way of education!

Yet in that which counts most, these two are born equal, for they have equal access to the God in themselves, equal chance to give Him means of expression. More than that, the God in one is just as powerful as the God in the other, for both are part of that all-powerful God of the Universe who rules the world.

In effect, we are each of us individual cells in the great Mind of the universe—the God Mind. We can draw upon the Mind of the Universe in exactly the same way that any cell in our own body draws upon our brain for whatever it needs outside its immediate surroundings.

All men are born free and equal, just as all the cells in your body are equal. Some of these cells may seem to be more fortunately situated than others, being placed in fatty portions of the body where they are so surrounded with nourishment that they seem assured of everything they can need for their natural lives.

Others may be in hard-worked parts where they are continually having to draw upon the lymph around them, and through it upon the blood stream and the heart, and where it seems as though they cannot be sure of sustenance from one day to the next. Still others may be in little-used and apparently forgotten parts where they seem to have been left to dry up and starve, as in the scalp of the head when the hair falls out and the fatty tissue of the scalp dries, leaving the cells there to shrivel and die.

Yet despite their apparent differences in surroundings and opportunity, all these cells are equal, all can draw upon every element in the body for sustenance at need.

To see how it is done, let us take a single nerve cell in our own brain, and see how it works.

Look up the diagram of a typical nerve cell in any medical work, and what do you find? From one side of the cell, a long fibre extends which makes connection with some part of the skin, or some group of cells such as a muscle. This fibre is part of the nerve cell. It is the telephone line, carrying orders or stimuli from the cell to the muscle it controls, or from the sensory nerve in the skin to the cell in the brain. Thoughts, emotions, desires, all send impulses to the nerves controlling the muscles concerned, and provide the stimuli which set these muscles in action, thus transforming nervous energy into muscular energy.

So if you have a desire which requires the action of only a single muscle, what happens? Your desire takes the form of an impulse to the nerve cell controlling that muscle, the order travels along the cell-fibre to the muscle, which promptly acts in accord with the stimulus given it. And your desire is satisfied.

But suppose your desire requires the action of more than one muscle? Suppose it needs the united power of every muscle in the body? So far we have used only the long nerve fibre or telephone line connecting the nerve cell with the muscle it controls. But on the other side of each nerve cell are short fibres, apparently ending in space. And as long as the nerves are at rest, these fibres do lie in space.

But when you stir up the nerve cells, when you give them a job that is greater than the muscles at their command can manage, then these short fibres go into action. Then they bestir themselves to some purpose. They dig into the nerve cells near them. They wake these and stimulate them in turn to stir up those on the other sides of them until, if necessary, every cell in the brain is twitching, and every muscle in the body working to accomplish the job you command.

That is what happens in *your* body if even a single cell in your brain desires something strongly enough, persistently enough, to hold to its purpose until it gets what it wants. And that is what happens in the God-body when you put the same persistence into your desires.

You see, you are a cell in the God-body of the Universe, just as every cell in you is a part of your body. When you work with your hands, your feet, your muscles, you are using only the muscles immediately connected with your brain cells. When you work with the money you have, the riches or friends or influence you control, you are using only the means immediately connected to your brain cell in the mind of God. And that is so infinitesimally small a part of the means and resources at the command of that Great God-mind.

It is just as though you tried to do all the work required of your body today by using only the tiniest muscle in your little finger, when by stirring up the surrounding nerve cells, you could just as well draw upon the power of the whole mind, or of the entire body if that were needed. It is as though one of your nerve cells undertook to do the work of the whole body, and tried, with the single muscle at its command, to do it!

You'd think that foolish, if one tiny nerve cell out of the billions in your brain, undertook any such gigantic job. You'd know it was hopeless ... that no one cell, and no one muscle, could ever accomplish all that work. Yet you, as a single cell in the God-mind, have often attempted just as impossible jobs. When all you had to do to accomplish everything you desired was to stir into action the cells around you!

How can you do this? In the same way that any cell in your own brain does it. *Pray!* In other words, get an urgent, insistent desire. The first principle of success is DESIRE— knowing what you want. Desire is the planting of your seed. It needs cultivation, of course, but the first important step is the PLANTING. Desire stirs the nerve cells in your brain to use the muscles under their control to do the work required of them. Desire will set your nerve cell in the God-mind vibrating, using the muscle under its command and stirring into action all the nerve cells around it until they, too, are working with you to bring about the thing you wish.

That is the reason it was said in the Vedas thousands of years ago that if any two people would unite their psychic forces, they could conquer the world! That is the reason Jesus told us—"If two of you shall agree as touching anything they shall ask, it shall be done unto them. For when two or three are gathered together in My name, there am I in the midst of them, and I shall grant their request."

When two or more nerve cells unite for a certain action, they get that action, even if to bring it about they have to draw upon every cell in the whole body for help!

This does not mean that anything is impossible to a single cell or a single person—merely that 'when two or more are united for a common purpose, the results are easier. But there is no good thing any man can ask, believing, that he cannot get.

In the first chapter of Genesis, it is written that God gave man dominion over the earth. And it is true. It is just as true as that any nerve cell in your whole body has dominion over your body. If you doubt it, let one nerve be sufficiently irritated, and see how quickly it puts every nerve in your body to work to remove that irritation.

One nerve cell in your body, with a strongly held purpose, can bring into action every cell in your body to accomplish that purpose. One nerve cell in the God-body (in other words, one man or woman) with a strongly held purpose, can bring into action every cell in the Universe, if these be necessary to the accomplishment of that purpose!

Does that mean anything to you? Does it mean anything to know that the words of prophets and seers are true, that the promises of the Scriptures can be depended upon, that there really is a Power in the Universe that responds to the urge of the lowliest man or woman just as readily as to the command of the highest?

The world is yours! It matters not whether you be prince or pauper, blue-blooded or red, white-skinned, black, yellow or brown. The God-body of the Universe makes no more distinction between cells than do you in responding to the impulses of the nerve cells in your own body.

Rich or poor—it's all one to you. Highly placed or low—one can cause you as much trouble, or give you as great satisfaction, as another. And the same is true of the God-body of the Universe. All men are created free and equal. All remain free and equal nerve cells in the God-mind of the Universe.

The only difference lies in our understanding of the power that is ours. How much understanding have you? And what are you doing to increase it? "Seek first understanding, and all things else shall be added unto you." Easier to believe that now, isn't it? With the right understanding, you could run the world. Can you think of anything more important than acquiring understanding?

What turned the complaining, discouraged, poverty-stricken and quite ordinary young Bonaparte into the greatest military genius of his age, "Man of Destiny" and master of most of Europe?

The Talisman of Napoleon, the Talisman of every great and successful man, the only Talisman that will stir the whole body of the Universe into action, is the same Talisman as that needed to put the entire physical body at the service of any one nerve cell—*a purpose so strongly held that life or death or anything else seems of small consequence beside it!* A purpose— and the persistent determination to hold to it until it is accomplished.

Love sometimes makes such a Talisman—the love that goes out to dare all and do all for the loved one. Greed oftentimes brings it into being—hence many of the great fortunes of today. The lust for power is a potent Talisman, that has animated men since time began. Greater still is the zeal of one who would convert the world. That Talisman has carried men through fire and flood, into every danger and over every obstacle. Look how Mohammed, a lowly camel driver, became the ruler of and prophet to millions.

Faith in charms, belief in luck, utter confidence in another's leadership, all are Talismans of greater or lesser power.

But the greatest of all is belief in the God inside YOU! Belief in its power to draw to itself every element it needs for expression. Belief in a definite PURPOSE it came here to fulfill, and which can be fulfilled only through YOU!

Have you such a faith? If not, get it! For without such a faith, life is purposeless, meaningless. What is more, until you lay hold of that Talisman, life will never bring anything worth while to you!

What was it won for Grant over his more brilliant opponents? The grim, dogged, persistent purpose to fight it out along those lines if it

took all summer! What is it that has made England victor in so many of
her wars, in spite of inept leadership and costly blunders? That same
bull-dog determination, which holds on in spite of all reverses and discouragements, until its fight is won. What was it that wore out the
unjust judge, in the parable that Jesus told?

And he spake a parable unto them to this end, that man ought always
to pray, and not to faint; saying, "There was in a city a judge, which
feared not God, neither regarded man;

"And there was a widow in that city; and she came unto him, saying,
'Avenge me on mine adversary'

"And he would not for a while; but afterward he said within himself,
'Though I fear not God, nor regard man; yet because this widow
troubleth me, I will avenge her, lest by her continual coming she weary
me.'"

And the Lord said, "Hear what the unjust judge saith. And shall not
God avenge his own elect, which cry day and night unto him, though
he bear long with them?"

If the nerve in a tooth keeps crying out that a cavity in that tooth
needs attention, won't you finally drop everything and seek out a dentist
who can satisfy that nerve's needs? And if any other nerve prays
continuously for attention, won't you do likewise with it?

Well, you are a nerve in the God-body. If you have an urgent need,
and keep praying and insisting and demanding the remedy, don't you
suppose you will get it just as surely?

A definite purpose, held to in the face of every discouragement and
failure, in spite of all obstacles and opposition, will win no matter what
the odds. It is the one nerve cell working against the indifference, the
inertia or even the active opposition of the entire group. If the cell is
easily discouraged, it will fail. If it is willing to wait indefinitely it will
have to wait. But if it keeps stirring up the cells next to it, and
stimulating them to stir those beyond, eventually the entire nerve system
will go into action and bring about the result that single cell
desires—even if it be only to rid itself of the constant irritation.

You have seen young fellows determined to go to college. You have
thought them foolish, in the face of the obstacles facing them. Yet when

they persisted, you know how often those obstacles have one by one magically disappeared, until presently they found themselves with the fruition of their desires. A strongly held purpose, persisted in, believed in, is as sure to win in the end as the morrow's sun is to rise. And earnest prayer is to the God-body what a throbbing nerve is to yours. Hold to it, insist upon it, and it is just as sure of a hearing. But remember:

He that wavereth is like the wave of the sea, driven by the wind and tossed; yet not that man think that he shall receive anything of the Lord.

All are born free and equal. All may not start with the same amount of wealth or opportunity immediately available to them, but all can go to the Source of these and get just as much of them as is necessary to satisfy their desires.

We are surrounded by riches. We have available unlimited wealth. But we have to learn how to draw it to us.

Years ago, at Kimberley in South Africa, a poor Boer farmer tried to glean a living out of the rocky soil. His boys oftentimes picked up pieces of dirty-looking crystal and used them as pebbles to throw at some wandering sheep. After years of fruitless effort, the farmer abandoned his attempts to make a living out of this rocky soil, and moved to a more fertile spot. Today, the farm he tried so hard to cultivate is the site of the Kimberley Diamond Mines, one of the richest spots on the face of the globe. And the bits of dirty crystal that his boys threw at the sheep turned out to be diamonds in the rough!

Most of us are like that poor Boer farmer. We strive and struggle, and frequently give up, because of ignorance of our powers, ignorance of the good things around us. We remain in poverty until along comes someone and shows that we were standing on a diamond mine all the time.

Russell Conwell tells the story of a Pennsylvania farmer whose brother went to Canada and became an oil driller. Fired with the brother's tales of sudden wealth, the farmer sold his land and went to Canada to make his fortune. The new owner, in looking over the farm, found that where the cattle came to drink from a little creek, a board had been put across the water to hold back a heavy scum which was washed down by the rains from the ground above.

He examined this scum, and thought it smelled like oil. So he had some experts come out and look the ground over. It proved to be one of the richest oil fields in the state of Pennsylvania.

What riches are you overlooking? What opportunities? Opportunity," says a famous writer, "is like oxygen. It is so plentiful that we fairly breathe it." All that is necessary is a receptive mind, a willingness to try, and the persistence to see things through.

There is some one thing that YOU can do better than anyone else. There is some line of work in which you can excel—if you will just find that one thing and spend all your time and effort in learning to do it supremely well.

Don't worry if it seems to be some humble thing that anyone ought to be able to do. In a magazine some time ago, there was the story of a Polish immigrant who could speak scarcely a word of English, who had no trade or training and had to take any sort of job that offered. He happened to get one in a nursery, digging up dirt for the flowers. He dug so well that soon he was attending to the planting of many of the commoner varieties of flowers.

Among these were the peonies. He loved those big peonies, gave them such careful attention that they thrived and grew more beautiful than ever. Soon his peonies began to attract attention, the demand for them grew, until he had to double and then quadruple the space devoted to them. Today he is half owner of that nursery.

Two artists opened an office together, doing any kind of work they could get. One noticed that wherever he happened to do cartoons for people, the results were so effective that they came back for more. So he made an especial study of cartoon drawing. Today his earnings are in the $25,000 class, while his fellow artist is still barely making ends meet as a jack of all trades.

A retail clerk found that she had a special gift for satisfying complaining customers. She liked to straighten out the snarls that others had caused, and she did it so well that she soon attracted the attention of her employers. Today she is head of the complaint department.

There is the switchboard operator with the pleasing voice, the reception clerk with the cheery smile, the salesman with the convincing manner, the secretary with the knack of saving the boss' time, the drummer with the jolly manner. Every one of us has something. Find out what one thing you can do best, cultivate it and you can be the biggest man in that line in the world.

Success is where you are and within yourself. Don't try to imitate what someone else is doing. Develop what YOU have. There is something in you that will enable you to reach the top in some one line. Put the spot light on your own characteristics, your own abilities. Find what you can do best, what people like you best for. Then cultivate that.

When the great Comstock Lode was first discovered, a fortune was taken out of it. Then the ore petered out. The owners presently gave up and sold out to a new group. These men spent several hundred thousand dollars in a fruitless attempt to locate the rich lode, and they too were ready to give up. But someone thought to try a bore hole to the side of one of the entries, and struck an almost solid mass of ore so rich that nearly $300,000,000 was taken from it.

In the early days of the prairie farms, newcomers were frequently able to buy for a song the homesteads of the original settlers, because the latter had been able to find no water. They had dug wells, but had been unable to reach the streams beneath. Oftentimes, however, by digging only a few feet further, the newcomers found water in abundance. The first settlers had quit when success was almost within their grasp. The greatest success usually comes from one step beyond the point where defeat overtook you. "He who loses wealth, loses much," says an old proverb. "He who loses a friend, loses more. But he who loses his courage, loses everything."

Three things educators try to instil into children:

> 1st—Knowledge
> 2nd—Judgment
> 3rd—Persistence.

And the greatest of these is Persistence. Many a man has succeeded without education. Many even without good judgment. But none has ever got anywhere worth while without persistence. Without a strong desire, without that inner urge which pushes him on, over obstacles, through discouragements, to the goal of his heart's desire.

"Nothing in the world can take the place of persistence," said Calvin Coolidge. "Talent will not. Nothing is more common than unsuccessful men with talent. Genius will not; unrewarded genius is almost a proverb. Education will not; the world is full of educated derelicts. Persistence and determination alone are omnipotent. The slogan 'Press on' has solved and always will solve the problems of the human race."

Russell Conwell, the famous educator and lecturer who founded Temple University, gathered statistics some years ago on those who succeed, and his figures showed that of 4043 multimillionaires in this country at that time, only 69 had even a High School education. They lacked money, they lacked training, but they had the URGE to get somewhere, the *persistence* to keep trying ... and they succeeded!

Compare that with the figures Conwell gathered on the sons of rich men. Only one in seventeen died wealthy! Lacking incentive, having no urge within them to get ahead, they not only failed to make their mark, but they lost what they had.

The first essential of success is a feeling of lack, a need, a *desire* for something you have not got. It is the powerlessness of the cripple or invalid that makes him long for strength, gives him the necessary persistence to work for it until he gets it. It is the poverty and misery of their existence that makes the children of the Ghetto long for wealth, and gives them the persistence and determination to work at anything until they get it.

You need that same urgent desire, that same determination and persistence if you are to get what you want from life. You need to realize that whatever it is you want of life, it is there for the taking. You need to know that you are a cell in the God-mind, and that through this God-mind you can put the whole Universe to work, if necessary, to bring about the accomplishment of your desire.

But don't waste that vast power on trifles. Don't be like the fable of the woodsman who, having worked long and hard for the wishing Fairy and accomplished the task she set him, was told that he might have in reward any three things he asked for. Being very hungry, he promptly asked for a good meal. That eaten, he noticed that the wind was blowing up cold, so he asked for a warm cloak. With his stomach full and a warm cloak about him, he felt sleepy, so he asked for a comfortable bed to lie upon.

And so, with every good thing of the world his for the asking, the next day found him with only a warm cloak to show for his labors. Most of us are like that. We put the mountain in labor, just to bring forth a mouse. We strive and strain, and draw upon all the powers that have been given us, to accomplish some trifling thing that leaves us just where we were before.

Demand much! Set a worth-while goal. Remember the old poem by Jessie B. Rittenhouse from "The Door of Dreams" published by Houghton Mifflin Co., Boston.

> *I bargained with Life for a penny*
> *And Life would pay no more,*
> *However I begged at evening*
> *When I counted my scanty store.*
>
> *For Life is a just employer;*
> *He gives you what you ask,*
> *But once you have set the wages,*
> *Why, you must bear the task.*
>
> *I worked for a menial's hire,*
> *Only to learn, dismayed,*
> *That any wage I had asked of Life,*
> *Life would have paid.*

Don't you be foolish like that. Don't bargain with Life for a penny. Ask for something worth putting the Universe to work for. Ask for it, demand it—then stick to that demand with persistence and determination until the whole God-mind HAS to bestir itself to give you what you want.

The purpose of Life from the very beginning has been dominion—dominion over every adverse circumstance. And through his part of dominion, his nerve cell in the Mind of God and his ability through it to get whatever action he may persistently demand—man HAS dominion over everything.

There is a Spark of Divinity in YOU. What are you doing to fan it into flame? Are you giving it a chance to grow, to express itself, to become an all-consuming fire? Are you giving it work to do? Are you making it seek out ever greater worlds to conquer? Or are you letting it slumber neglected, or perhaps even smothering it with doubt and fear?

And God said, Let us make man in our image, after our likeness; and let him have DOMINION over the fish of the sea, and over the fowl of the air, and over the cattle, and over all the earth, and over every creeping thing that creepeth upon the earth.

Do you know what is the Unpardonable Sin in all of Nature? Read the following chapters, and you will see!

Affirmation:

And every morning I will say, There's something happy on the way. And God sends love to me. God is the light of my life, the Source of my knowledge and inspiration. God in the midst of me knows. He provides me with food for my thoughts, ideas for excellent service, clear perception, Divine intelligence.

THE GOAL OF LIFE

Mind is the Master-power that moulds and makes,
And Man is Mind, and evermore he takes
The tool of Thought, and, shaping what he wills,
Brings forth a thousand joys, a thousand ills:—
He thinks in secret, and it comes to pass:
Environment is but his looking glass.

—JAMES ALLEN

"In the beginning God created the heaven and earth. And the earth was without form and void; and dark ness was upon the face of the deep. And the Spirit of God moved upon the face of the waters. And God said ..."

In the beginning was Mind, Energy, without form, without direction . . . like so much static electricity. Then came the Word, the mental image, to make all that power dynamic, to give it form and direction. What matters it the form it took first, so long as it had definite direction? It required an Intelligence to give it shape. That is the first great fact of the Scriptures. NOT that the heavens and earth were created, or light brought forth, but that *any form presupposes a Directing Intelligence!*

You cannot have dynamic electricity without a generator—an intelligence to conceive and direct it. No more can you have an earth or a flower, without an Intelligence to give them form from the static energy all about.

In the beginning, not merely was the earth without form and void, but the whole universe was the same way. Just as the interspaces of the universe are today. Everything was static—energy in flux. But "the Spirit of God moved upon the face of the waters. And God said, Let there be light."

St. John puts it—"In the beginning was the Word. And the Word was with God. And the Word was God." And what is the "Word"? As often mentioned before, a word is not a mere sound issuing from the lips, or so many letters written by hand. A word is a mental concept, an idea, an image.

In the beginning was the mental image! Read over that first chapter of Genesis, and you will see that in everything God created, the "Word" came first—then the material form. The "Word" had to come first—you cannot build a house without first having a clear image of the house you are going to build. You cannot make anything, without first conceiving a mental image of the thing to be created. Not even God could do that!

So when God said—"Let the earth bring forth grass," He had in mind a clear mental picture of what grass was like. As the Scriptures put it—"The Lord God made the earth and the heavens, and every plant of the field *before it was in the earth,* and every herd of the field *before it grew."* First the "Word," the mental image—then the creation.

It requires intelligence to form a mental concept. The animals cannot do it. They can recall images of things they have seen. They cannot conceive concepts from pure ideas. So, as stated above, creation pre-supposes a mental image, and a mental image means a directing Intelligence behind it.

That is the first conclusion that a reading of the Scriptures forces upon us. And the second is that like reproduces like.

Go over that first chapter again, and you will find that no less than six different times is the assertion repeated that "everything reproduces after its kind …" "Let the earth bring forth grass, the herb yielding seed, and the fruit tree yielding fruit *after his kind,* whose seed is in itself…. Let the earth bring forth the living creature after his kind, cattle, and creep-ing thing, and beast of the earth after his kind."

Then God made man in His own image, after His likeness. Notice that! After telling us repeatedly that everything reproduced after its own kind, the Scriptures go on to say that God made man *in His own image.* That can mean only one thing—that man, too, is a God! For throughout all nature, hybrids are sterile. Nothing can breed out of its own kind. Different races, different strains of the same species, can interbreed, but all must be of the same kind.

So when God made man in His own image, and bade him be fruitful and multiply, He thereby showed that man was no hybrid, but of the true breed of God. And to prove it, he gave man dominion over the "fish of the sea, and over the fowl of the air, and over every living thing that moveth upon the earth." And He bade man replenish the earth, *and subdue it,* and have dominion.

Simple instructions, and easily carried out—in part— but as for subduing the earth, and having dominion over it, mankind is still in the primer class. Yet if man is a God— *and he is*—then he *can* do it. And anything so worthwhile as that is worth all our effort to learn how to do.

For if we are gods and true sons of God—as the Scriptures frequently assure us—then we must possess all the properties of God. We must be creators. Then why don't we create happier conditions? Why don't we do away with poverty and disease and all unhappiness?

Why? Because it takes understanding and faith to use our powers, and so few have the patience to work for them. Men will study for years to become doctors, or lawyers, or engineers. And they will start the practice of their professions in fear and trembling, realizing that it will be years before they will have gained enough practical knowledge from experience to be really competent in their work.

Yet they will read a book or two on psychology or some of the mental sciences, and if they cannot put the principles into practice next day, they give up in disgust and condemn the principles as tommyrot!

Of all fields of study, none offers such possibilities as the study of the inner powers of man. None offers such sure rewards to the persevering, sincere student. Yet there is no field so neglected by the average man. Nine men out often—yes, ninety-nine out of a hundred—merely drift through life. With generators inside them capable of producing power enough to accomplish any purpose, they get nowhere.

They use their generators, of course, but to what purpose? To sigh over some movie idol—or thrill over the exploits of some notorious racketeer—or wax indignant at the thieving of a fat city grafter. Vicarious emotions, all of them—yet because it is so much easier to enjoy one's thrills vicariously, most people go through life experiencing few others.

They speed up their generators, but with no resultant good to themselves. Their experiences are all dream pictures. When they leave the movies, or put down their paper or book, they wake up! They never make the effort necessary to bring those thrills into their own lives.

Suppose the envelope of air that surrounds the globe were a great storage battery of electrical energy. Every thought, every fervent desire, every emotion, adds to the energy there. Every time you run your generator—with feelings of love or hate or fear or envy or hope or faith—you put additional energy into that storage battery.

But to draw energy out of this storage battery, you must have good conductors, good wires, the wires of a definite purpose, strongly held. And to keep the energy from dissipating requires the insulation of faith.

You cannot get much current from a storage battery by merely touching your wires to its posts, letting them slip on and off continuously. You have to twist them securely around the posts, fasten them there firmly with the screw cap, to get a constant current.

And you cannot use plain wires, or the current will run off into the first conductor that comes in contact with it. Your wires must be insulated, so the current will go directly from the battery to the appliance you wish it to run.

It is the same with the storage battery of power all around you. You can draw upon it at will, you can get flashes of power from it at the touch of fervent prayer or under the stress of any other high emotion, but if you want a continuous flow of power, you must have first a firmly held purpose, then the insulation of serene faith. Given these, there is no limit to the power you can draw, or the purposes to which it can be put.

Now how would this help if you were out of a job, had a wife and children waiting for something to eat, a home that was about to be taken away from you—and you had been praying and trying in every way you knew to raise the necessary money? How could you use the idea? What would you need to do?

Remember, in the Bible, how it is told that the apostles labored all night long, and caught nothing, yet when Jesus bade them cast their nets on the right side, and they did so, their nets were filled to overflowing?

You have been praying and trying, and you have caught nothing. Now it is your turn to cast your nets on the right side. And casting them there means to disregard the material world around you for a moment, and do your fishing in the world of energy!

All around you is energy—unappropriated energy that you can turn into any form you wish. The same flux out of which God created the world! And you are a god, a creator, a true son of the Father. You have the same power to make of your world what you like that He has. It requires only the same method He used.

First, the "Word," the mental image. What is it you want? Position, power, love, riches, success? Make your mold. The best flux in the world will not make a usable shape unless you have a mold to pour it in. So make your mold, your mental image. See it clearly in your mind's eye. Don't make it the home or position or riches that belong to someone else. Use them as a model, if you like, but make your own out of virgin material.

Second, the flux. "The Spirit of God moved on the face of the waters." Throw your net, your spirit, around as much of the unappropriated energy about as you need to fill your mold. Then hold to it with the dogged grip of the bulldog. It is yours. You have filed your claim upon it, and no one can take it away from you unless you weaken and let go. Hold to that knowledge with grim, unshakable purpose, and there is nothing you cannot get.

"Whatsoever you ask for when you pray, believe that you receive it, and you shall have it." Whatever you want, make your mental hold, then throw your net around the flux necessary to fill it, and hold on to it until that flux has hardened. It is yours. You *have* it. You have only to believe, to *know that you have it*, in order to give that flux time to harden so that all can see it.

But to lose faith is to pull away the mold while your flux is still liquid. It will run like quicksilver in all directions, and you have to start all over again, making a new mold, casting your net around new energy, starting again to give it time to harden and become manifest.

In every man there is a Seed of Life, with infinite power to draw to itself whatever it conceives to be necessary to its expression. It doesn't matter who you are, what your environment or education or advantages, the Seed of Life in you has the same power for good.

What is it makes a poor immigrant-boy like Edward Bok, overcome every handicap of language and education, to become one of the greatest editors the country has known?

What is it accounts for the fact that, as before-mentioned, of 4043 multimillionaires in this country a few years before the first World War, all but 69 started so poor that they had not even a high school education?

Isn't it that the more circumstances conspire to repress it, the stronger becomes the urge of the Life in you for expression? The more it lacks channels through which to expand, the more inclined it is to burst its shell and flow forth in all directions?

It is the old case of the river that is dammed, generating the most power. Most of us are so placed that some opportunity for expression is made easy for us. And that little opportunity serves like a safety valve to a boiler—it leaves us steam enough to do something worth while, yet keeps us from getting up enough power to burst the shell about us, and sweep away every barrier that holds us down.

Yet it is only such an irresistible head of steam as that which makes great successes. That is why the blow which knocks all the props from under us is often the turning point in our whole career. Take the case of a man I know who, five years after losing his job, reached his goal as head of a rival company and the greatest authority on his product in the country. Do you suppose he would ever have won these rewards had he continued as salesman for his original company?

No, indeed! He was getting along too well. He had a comfortable home, a fine family, a good income and congenial working conditions. Why should he disturb them? The old fable of the dog with the bone looking at his reflection in the water, keeps many a man from taking a chance at a better opportunity when he has a reasonably good one within his grasp. He's afraid he may be giving up the real for the chimera.

Yet playing safe is probably the most unsafe thing in the world. You cannot stand still. You must go forward—or see the world slide past you.

This was well illustrated by figures worked out by one of the big Economic Services. Of all those who have money at 35, 87% lose it by the time they are 60.

Why?—Because the fortunes they have take away the need for initiative on their part. Their money gives to them easy means of expressing the urge in them, without effort on their part. It gives them dozens of safety valves, through which their steam continually escapes.

The result is that they not only accomplish nothing worth while, but they soon dissipate the fortunes that were left them. They are like kettles, the urge of life keeping the water at boiling point, but the open spout of ease letting the steam escape as fast as it forms, until presently there is not even any water left.

Why do the sons of rich men so seldom accomplish anything worth while? Because they don't have to. Every opportunity is given them to express the urge in them through pleasant channels, and they dissipate through these the energies that might carry them to any height. The result? They never have a strong enough "head of steam" left to carry through any real job.

With us ordinary mortals, however, sooner or later comes a crisis in our affairs, and how we meet it determines our future happiness and success. Since the beginning of time, every form of life has been called upon to meet such crises. So the goal of life has always been DOMINION—a means of overcoming all obstacles, of winning dominion over circumstances.

In "Weekly Unity" Magazine, some years ago, there was the story of a couple who wanted to dispose of their house and move to another town. But the so-called "Depression" was on at that time, and houses were a drug on the market. Real Estate Agents held out no hope, so "Why not try prayer?"—a friend asked. "What can we lose?" they asked each other. So they sat down together and tried to realize—

1. That there is only one Mind, that they were parts of that Mind, and that those to whom they must sell were also parts of it.

2. That this God-Mind is working for the good of all—for their good and for that of those who were seeking just such a home as theirs.

3. That this God-Mind was glad to help them, glad to help those seeking such a home, so all they had to do was to put their home in His hands, and leave the working out of the problem confidently and serenely to Him.

Within a short time, they sold the house for a good price for CASH. In another issue, "Unity" told about a dealer who had bought a number of pianos on credit, and borrowed some of the money from the bank to pay for them. The pinch came, and the bank notified him that his note must be paid by a certain date. He went home worried and miserable. With the help of his wife, however, he was able to throw off the worry and put it up to the God Inside Him to find the necessary funds.

That afternoon, one of the clerks came to him and said there was a man cursing and swearing about something he had bought from him the day before. He went over to the man and found him ranting and raging about an inexpensive article he had purchased for his son, on which some of the strings had broken. The shopkeeper promptly gave him a better article to replace it. That took all the wind out of the complaining customer's sails, and he became so apologetic that he felt he had to buy something else to make up for his boorish behavior. It developed that he was planning to get a fine piano for his daughter's birthday, and the money he promptly paid for this proved to be more than enough to take care of the dealer's note at the bank.

The goal of life since the beginning of time has been DOMINION over just such circumstances as these, and only through the God in you can you win it. "My soul, wait thou only upon God," bade the prophet of old, "for my expectation is from Him."

But don't limit the channels through which His help can come to you. Don't insist that it should be through a legacy from some rich uncle, or a raise in your pay or the winning of some prize or order. Develop any channel that looks promising, but leave ALL the channels open. And then act as though *you already possessed the thing you want.*

Don't say—"When this bill is paid—or this crisis past—I shall feel so relieved." Instead, say—"I AM relieved, I feel so content and peaceful now that this load is off my shoulders."

How will you act when you get the thing you want? Well, act that way now, think that way—and before you know it, you will BE that way. Remember the lines by Ella Wheeler Wilcox—

> *Thought is a magnet; and the longed-for pleasure*
> *Or boon or aim or object is the steel;*
> *And its attainment hangs but on the measure*
> *Of what thy soul can feel.*

How would you conduct yourself if you full realized your one-ness with God, if you could truly believe that He is constantly offering you life, love and every good thing your heart can desire? Well, that is exactly what He is doing!

So act as if you already had the thing you want. Visualize it as yours. See the picture clearly in every detail in your mind's eye. Then LET GOD make it manifest. Do what you can, of course, with what you have, where you are, but put your dependence upon God, and LET His good gifts come to you.

Look at the first chapter of the Scriptures. When God wanted light, did He strive and struggle, trying to make light? No, He said—*"Let* there be light."

When you want something very much, instead of trying to MAKE it come your way, suppose you try asking for it and then LETTING it come. Suppose you just relax, and *let* God work through you instead of trying to *make* Him do something for you. Suppose you say to yourself—"I will do whatever is given me to do. I will follow every lead to the best of my ability, but for the rest, it is all up to the God in me. God in me knows what my right work is, where it is, and just what I should do to get it. I put myself and my affairs lovingly in His hands, secure that whatever is for my highest good, He will bring to me."

Emerson used to say that when we discern Truth, we do nothing of ourselves but allow a passage for its beams. They express the same thought in electricity through the equation $-C = E\,/\,R$: The current delivered at any given point is equal to the voltage divided by the resistance. With too much resistance, no current is delivered, no matter how much may be available.

When we worry and are tense and fearful, we set up so great resistance that God finds it difficult to get through to us. We have to LET GO before we can become good conductors. Like John Burroughs, we must be able to say— "Serene I fold my hands and wait, nor care for wind or tide or sea. No more I strive against time or fate, for lo! Mine own shall come to me."

Unity has a favorite Prayer of Faith, written by Hannah More Kohaus, which all of us might well use when we are worried or sick or in need. If you will relax and repeat it slowly aloud, it is calculated to help you in any crisis:

> God IS MY help in every need;
> God does my every hunger feed;
> God walks beside me, guides my way
> Through every moment of the day.
>
> I now am wise, I now am true,
> Patient, kind, and loving, too.
> All things I am, can do, and be,
> Through Christ the Truth that is in me.
>
> God is my health, I can't be sick;
> God is my strength, unfailing, quick;
> God is my all; I know no fear,
> Since God and love and Truth are here.

A GOLDEN RULE MOTTO
> I shall pass through this world but once.
> Any good, therefore, that I can do
> Or any kindness that I can show
> To any human being Let me do it now. Let me
> Not defer it or neglect it for
> I shall not pass this way again.

—ANONYMOUS

ONLY A COG IN A WHEEL

A man there was of unusual gifts
Bearing an honored name,
Life came to him with outstretched hands
Proffering wealth and fame;
But he carelessly turned his head away,
The prize made little appeal,
Contenting himself with a minor part,
He was only a cog in a wheel.

When opportunity knocked at his door,
It found him asleep and deaf;
Long and patiently it waited there,
But he did not come to himself.
His golden chances were wasted like chaff,
He took no account of the real;
Each day a monotonous grind to him,
He was only a cog in a wheel.

In the image of God this man was made,
With power to do and to serve;
Strong of mind and body was he,
But he lacked essential nerve.
So he drifted along from day to day,
Without ambition or zeal,
Playing a dull and nondescript part,
He was only a cog in a wheel.

What place do you fill in life's great machine—
Are you using your gifts aright?
Today have you wrought some truly fine thing—
Can you claim to have fought a good fight?
Will it surely be said that you "played the game"—

That your life was productive and real?
Or will the world say, as it goes on its way,
He was only a cog in a wheel?

                                        —ANONYMOUS

Many versions as to the true description of Christ have been given to the world. Among the most authentic is this one, written by Publius Lentulus, President of Judea, to Tiberius Caesar, and first appeared in the writings of Saint Anselm of Canterbury in the Eleventh Century.

"There lived at this time in Judea a man of singular virtue—whose name is Jesus Christ whom the barbarians esteem as a prophet, but his followers love and adore him as the offspring of the immortal God. He calls back the dead from the graves and heals all sorts of diseases with a word or touch. He is a tall man, well shaped, and of an amiable and reverend aspect—his hair of a color that can hardly be matched, falling into graceful curls, waving about and very agreeably couched about his shoulders, parted on the crown of his head, running as a stream to the front after the fashion of the Nazarites; his forehead high, large and imposing; his cheeks without spot or wrinkle, beautiful with a lovely red; his nose and mouth formed with exquisite symmetry; his beard of a color suitable to his hair, reaching below his chin and parted in the middle like a fork; his eyes bright and blue, clear and serene, look innocent, dignified, manly and mature. Often times however, just before he reveals his divine powers, his eyelids are gently closed in reverential silence. In proportion of body most perfect and captivating; his arms and hands are delectable to behold. He rebukes with majesty, counsels with mildness, his whole address, whether in word or deed, being eloquent and grave. No man has seen him laugh, yet his manners are exceedingly pleasant, but he has wept frequently in the presence of men. He is temperate, modest and wise. A man for his extraordinary beauty and divine perfection, surpassing the children of men in every sense."

YOUR MENTAL BROWNIES

Mankind, like Ancient Gaul, can be divided into three parts.

1st—Those who are still in a state of simple consciousness, living, acting and thinking as the animals do. Men and women in this class can be said to exist— nothing more.

2nd—Those in a state of self-consciousness. This comprises the great bulk of the higher races of mankind. They reason, they study, they work, they sorrow and enjoy. But they are forced to depend for all good things upon their own efforts and they are subject to all manner of circumstances and conditions beyond their control. Theirs is a state of struggle.

3rd—Those entering into or who have reached the intuitional or higher consciousness, that state which Jesus termed the Kingdom of Heaven within us.

Just as, in the childhood of the race, there was brought forth an Adam and Eve with such advanced receptual intellects that they presently developed conceptual ideas (i.e. named impressions and the ability to classify them, compare them and draw conclusions from them), so today are to be found here and there the advance guard of the Mental Age—men and women as far ahead of the ordinary conceptual intellect of their fellows as this is in advance of the simple consciousness of the animal.

You see, the animal recognizes only images. Each house is to him a new house, with its own associations of food or famine, of kindness or blows. He never generalizes, or draws conclusions by comparing one house with another. His is the simple or receptual consciousness.

Man, on the other hand, takes his recept or image of a house and tabs it. He names it a house and then classifies it according to its kind. In that way, he turns it from a mere image into an idea or concept. It is as though he were traveling on a railroad train and keeping a tally of every house he passed. To the animal, it would mean filling his mind with the pictures of a hundred or more houses. To a man, it would be merely a matter of jotting down in the tablets of his memory—"100 houses, 25 of the Colonial type, 15 Tudor style, etc."

If his mind were too full of images, there would be no room in it to work out conclusions from those images, so man classifies those images into concepts or ideas, and thus increases his mental capacity a millionfold.

But now the time has come in his mental development when his mind is so full of concepts that a new short cut must be found. Here and there a few have already found this short cut and penetrated to the highest plane of consciousness—the intuitional or "Heaven" consciousness.

What is this higher consciousness? Bucke calls it the Cosmic Consciousness, and defines it as a consciousness of the world about us, a consciousness that does not have to stop and add concept to concept like a column of figures, but which can work out the answer immediately, intuitively, as a "lightning calculator" can work out a problem in mathematics, apparently without going through any of the intermediate stages of addition and subtraction, of labored reasoning from premise to conclusion.

You see, the conscious you is merely that aggregation of images and sensations and concepts known as the brain. But beyond and above this reasoning mind is your intuitive mind—the Soul of you—which is one cell in the great Oversoul of the Universe, God. It is the connecting link between God and you. It is part of Him. It shares in all His attributes, all His power and wisdom and riches. And at need it can draw upon the whole of these. How? In the same way that any cell of your body can draw upon the vitality of the whole body—by creating the need, *by using what it has.*

There is nothing mysterious about the way life works. It is all a logical growth. In the intellect, the young child first registers impressions, then it recognizes and tabs them, finally classifying them and using them as the basis for reasoning out ideas. By the use of impressions and images, the child can know the world it sees and feels. By concepts, it can construct in imagination the world it has not seen. Is this all? Is it the end?

"No!" answers Bucke in "Cosmic Consciousness." "As life arose in a world without life; as simple consciousness came into existence where before was mere vitality without perception; as self-consciousness soared forth over land and sea; so shall the race of man which has been thus established make other steps and attain to a yet higher life than any heretofore experienced or even conceived.

And let it be clearly understood that the new step is not merely an expansion of self-consciousness, but as distinct from it as that it's from simple consciousness, or as is this last from mere vitality without any consciousness at all.

But how shall we know this new sense? How recognize its coming? The signs are evident in every man and woman of high mentality. You have seen accountants who could write down a column of figures and give you the total without consciously adding one to another. You can recall instances when you have anticipated word for word what someone was about to say to you, when you have answered the telephone and known before he spoke who was at the other end of the wire, when you have met a stranger and formed a "snap judgment" of him which afterwards turned out to be marvelously correct. We call this intuition. It is the first stage of the Cosmic Consciousness. It is a perfectly logical step in the growth of the intellect.

In the jump from Simple Consciousness to Self-Consciousness, man combined groups of recepts or images into one concept or idea, just as we combine the three Roman numerals III into the one symbol 3. No longer did he have to hold in his mind each individual tree in a forest. He grouped them all together under one heading of trees, and called the group a forest.

Now he is advancing a step farther. Instead of having to first study each tree individually to learn the properties of that forest, he is getting that knowledge from the soul within him, which is part of the great Oversoul of the forest and of the Universe, and therefore knows all things. In other words, he is getting it intuitively.

That is the first step in reaching the Heaven consciousness—to cultivate your intuitions, to encourage them in every possible way. Your soul is a cell in the great God-body just as every cell in your body is part of you. And as part of the Oversoul of the Universe, it has access to all the knowledge of the Universe. But it needs exercise, it requires development.

When you want to develop any cell or set of cells in your body, what do you do? You exercise them, do you not? You use them to the limit of their abilities. Then what happens? They feel weak, exhausted. They become thin and emaciated. Why? Because you have broken up those cells, used the energy in them, and they have not yet had time to draw upon the blood stream for more. For the first few days or weeks that you continue that hard usage, they remain weak and nerveless. Again why? Because the amount of energy your "governor" is accustomed to apportioning those cells is not sufficient for such heavy work. But keep persevering, and what happens? Those cells not only harden until they are equal to any call you can make upon them, but they grow in size and power. They have put in a permanent order upon the "governor" for more life-giving energy, and as long as they can find use for it, that energy will keep coming to them.

That is the first thing you must do to grow in intuitive consciousness— cultivate what you have, use it on every possible occasion even though you seem to strain it beyond its powers at first. Listen for that still, small voice. And listen *to* it. "And thine ears shall hear a word behind thee," promised the Prophet of old, "saying—This is the way, walk ye in it, when ye turn to the right hand, and when ye turn to the left."

What is the vision of the artist, the inspiration of the writer, the discovery of the chemist or inventor, but his intuitive consciousness at work? Ask almost any great author, and he will tell you that he does not work out his plots. They "come to him"—that's all. "The key to successful methods," says Thomas A. Edison, "comes right out of the air. A real new thing like a general idea, a beautiful melody, is pulled out of space—a fact which is inexplicable."

Inexplicable—yes, from the viewpoint of the conceptual intellect—but quite understandable from the intuitive point of view.

So much for the first step. It is one possible to any man or woman of high intellect. When it involves a problem or a work of art or a story or a new discovery, it requires only filling the mind with all available concepts related to the desired result, then putting it up to the God in you to work out the answer.

The second step is the earnest desire for a higher consciousness. That sounds simple enough. Everybody would like to be able to learn without going through all the labor of adding percept to recept, making concepts of these and then figuring out the answers. So if the earnest desire is all that is needed, it ought to be easy.

Yet it is not. It is the hardest step of all. Why? Because the desire must be your *dominant* desire. It must not be merely a means to the end of obtaining riches or winning to high position.

All agree on this: This Heaven consciousness comes only as the result of a tremendous desire for spiritual truth, and a hunger and thirst after things of the spirit.

Perhaps that can be better understood when you remember how many ordinary people have had partial glimpses of it when almost at the point of death, or when coming out from under the influence of anaesthetics.

What, then, are the necessary conditions?

First, an understanding of the power latent in you, an understanding that, regardless of how much or how little education you have received, there is in you a power (call it the subconscious, or your soul, or your good genii or what you will) capable of contacting the Intelligence which directs and animates all of the universe.

Second, the earnest desire for spiritual growth. To possess this, a man need not be an ascetic, or give up his family or his business. In fact, he should be the better husband and father and business man for it. For the man of business today is no longer engaged in cheating his neighbor before the neighbor can cheat him. He is trying to *serve,* and to the extent that he succeeds in giving more and better service than others, he succeeds. Can you conceive of any finer preparation for the Heaven consciousness?

Third, the ability to thoroughly relax. As Boehme put it—"To cease from all thinking and willing and imaging. Your own 'self-conscious' hearing and willing and seeing hinder you from seeing and hearing God."

"When a new faculty appears in a race," says Bucke, "it will be found in the very beginning in one individual of that race; later it will be found in a few individuals; after a further time, in a larger percentage of the members of the race; still later, in half the members; and so on until, after thousands of generations, an individual who misses having the faculty is regarded as a monstrosity."

The Heaven consciousness, or Cosmic Consciousness as Bucke calls it, has reached the point of being found in many individuals. When a faculty reaches that point, it is susceptible of being acquired by all of the higher type of members of that race *who have reached full maturity.*

And it is never too late to develop this Intuitive Consciousness, for your mind never grows old. In his book, "The Age of Mental Virility," Dr. Dorland points out that more than half of mankind's greatest achievements were accomplished by men over 50 years old, and that more of these were done by men over 70 than by those under 30.

In tests made by Dr. Irving Lorge of Teachers College, Columbia University, it was found that while SPEED of learning might decline with years, the mental powers do not decline. When the speed penalty was eliminated, people of 50 and 60 made higher scores than those around 25. Dr. Lorge sums up his tests in these words:

As far as mental ability is concerned, there need be no "retiring age." The probabilities are that the older a person becomes, the more valuable he becomes. He possesses the same mental power he had in his young manhood, plus his wealth of experience and knowledge of his particular job. These are things that no youngster, however brilliant, can pick up.

You have an Intuitive Consciousness, which has evidenced itself many a time in "Hunches," and the like. Remains, then, only to develop it. Robert Louis Stevenson pointed the way when he told how he worked out the plot for Dr. Jekyll and Mr. Hyde.

"My Brownies! God bless them!" said Stevenson, "Who do one-half of my work for me when I am fast asleep, and in all human likelihood do the rest for me as well when I am wide awake and foolishly suppose that I do it myself. I had long been wanting to write a book on man's double being. For two days I went about racking my brains for a plot of any sort, and on the second night I dreamt the scene in Dr. Jekyll and Mr. Hyde at the window; and a scene, afterward split in two, in which Hyde, pursued, took the powder and underwent the change in the presence of his pursuer."

You have had similar experiences. You know how, after you have studied a problem from all angles, it sometimes seems worse jumbled than when you started on it. Leave it then for a while—forget it—and when you go back to it, you find your thoughts clarified, the line of reasoning worked out, your problem solved for you. It is your little "Mental Brownies" who have done the work for you!

The flash of genius does not originate in your own brain. Through intense concentration you have established a circuit through your subconscious mind with the Universal, and it is from IT that the inspiration comes. All genius, all progress, is from the same source. It lies with you merely to learn how to establish this circuit at will so that you can call upon IT at need. It can be done.

"There are many ways of setting the Brownies to work," says Dumont in "The Master Mind." "Nearly everyone has had some experience, more or less, in the matter, although often it is produced almost unconsciously, and without purpose and intent. Perhaps the best way for the average person—or rather the majority of persons—to get the desired results is for one to get as clear an idea of what one really wants to know—as clear an idea or mental image of the question you wish answered. Then after rolling it around in your mind—mentally chewing it, as it were—giving it a high degree of voluntary attention, you can pass it on to your Subconscious Mentality with the mental command: 'Attend to this for me—work out the answer!' or some similar order. This command may be given silently, or else spoken aloud—either will do. Speak to the Subconscious Mentality—or its little workers—just as you would speak to persons in your employ, kindly but firmly. Talk to the little workers, and firmly command them to do your work. And then forget all about the matter—throw it off your conscious mind, and attend to your other tasks. Then in due time will come your answer—flashed into your consciousness—perhaps not until the very minute that you must decide upon the matter, or need the information. You may give your Brownies orders to report at such and such a time—just as you do when you tell them to awaken you at a certain time in the morning so as to catch the early train, or just as they remind you of the hour of your appointment, if you have them all well trained."

Have you ever read the story by Richard Harding Davis of "The Man Who Could Not Lose?" In it the hero is intensely interested in racing.

He has studied records and "dope" sheets until he knows the history of every horse backward and forward.

The day before the big race he is reclining in an easy chair, thinking of the morrow's race, and he drops off to sleep with that thought on his mind. Naturally, his subconscious mind takes it up, with the result that he dreams the exact outcome of the race.

That was mere fiction, of course, but if races were run solely on the speed and stamina of the horses, it would be entirely possible to work out the results in just that way. Unfortunately, other factors frequently enter into every betting game.

But the idea behind Davis' story is entirely right. The way to contact your subconscious mind, the way to get the help of the "Man Inside You" in working out any problem is:

First, fill your mind with every bit of information regarding that problem that you can lay your hands on.

Second, pick out a chair or lounge or bed where you can recline in perfect comfort, where you can forget your body entirely.

Third, let your mind dwell upon the problem for a moment, not worrying, not fretting, but placidly, and then turn it over to the "Man Inside You." Say to him—"This is your problem. You Can do anything. You know the answer to everything. Work this out for me!" And utterly relax. Drop off to sleep, if you can. At least, drop into one of those half-sleepy, half-wakeful reveries that keep other thoughts from obtruding upon your consciousness. Do as Aladdin did— summon your Genie, give him your orders, then forget the matter, secure in the knowledge that he will attend to it for you. When you waken, *you will have the answer!*

"The smartest man in the world is the Man Inside," said Dr. Frank Crane. "By the Man Inside I mean that Other Man within each one of us that does most of the things we give ourselves credit for doing.

"I say he is the smartest man in the world. I know he is infinitely more clever and resourceful than I am or than any other man is that I ever heard of. When I cut my finger it is he that calls up the little phagocytes to come and kill the septic germs that might get into the wound and cause blood poisoning. It is he that coagulates the blood, stops the gash, and weaves the new skin.

"I could not do that. I do not even know how he does it. He even does it for babies that know nothing at all; in fact, does it better for them than for me.

"When I practice on the piano I am simply getting the business of piano playing over from my conscious mind to my subconscious mind: in other words, I am handing the business over to the Man Inside.

"Most of our happiness, as well as our struggles and misery, comes from this Man Inside. If we train him in ways of contentment, adjustment and decision, he will go ahead of us like a well-trained servant and do for us easily most of the difficult tasks we have to perform."

Read that last paragraph again. "Most of our happiness, *as well as our struggles and misery,* comes from this Man Inside."

How, then, can we use him to bring us only the good things of life?

By BLESSING instead of ranting and cursing, by TRUSTING instead of fearing. Every man is what he is because of the dominating thoughts that he permits to occupy his mind and thus suggests to the Man Inside.

Those thoughts that are mixed with some feeling of emotion, such as anger or fear or worry or love, magnetize that Man Inside and tend to drive him to such action as will attract to you similar or related thoughts and their logical reactions. All impulses of thought have a tendency to bring about their physical equivalent, simply because they set the Man Inside You to work trying to bring about the physical manifestations of your thought images. Jesus understood this when He said—"By their fruits shall ye know them."

What, then is the answer?

1. Realize that your thoughts are the molds in which the Man Inside You forms your circumstances, that "As a man thinketh, so is he."

2. Remember that there is nothing in all of God's Universe which you need to fear. For God is Love, and you are one with God. So make friends with your problems. Don't try to run away from

them. Walk up to them, bring them into the open, and you will find that they are not obstacles, but stepping-stones to something better.

3. If you are worrying or fearful, stop it. Put your affairs into the hands of the God in You—and forget them! Remember that all things are possible with God, and all things are possible with you when you

realize that you are one with Him. So look to God instead of to your difficulties. Look to the things you WANT—not to those you fear.

4. Forget the past. Remember—"Now is the accepted time. Now is the day of salvation." Look ahead to the great things that are before you—not backward at the regrets of the past. Look to what you want to see manifested. Think of each day as in itself a life, and say each morning—"I wake to do the work of a man."

5. Bless all things, for under even the most unprepossessing exterior lies a kernel of good. Remember that "When Fortune means to man most good, she looks upon him with a threatening eye."

In "Unity Weekly," the story is told of a farmer who, when he plows a field, blesses every seed he puts into it, and visualizes the abundant harvest it will bring. His neighbors marvel at the size of his crops.

In another issue, they tell of a guest in a western hotel who was impressed by the atmosphere of joy and peace in the room she occupied. Living in it seemed to be an inspiration. She was so filled with the presence of good in it that she asked the maid who had occupied it before, to give it such a restful atmosphere. The maid told her it was not the occupant, but herself; that whenever she worked in a room she blessed it, and as she left it, she stood in the door for a moment affirming peace and restfulness for it and blessing for the one who would occupy it.

Arthur Guiterman has written a blessing for every home that each of us might well use:

> *Bless the four corners of this house,*
> *And be the Lintel blest;*
> *And bless the hearth, and bless the board,*
> *And bless each place of rest;*
> *And bless the door that opens wide*
> *To stranger, as to kin;*
> *And bless each crystal windowpane*
> *That lets the starlight in;*
> *And bless the rooftree overhead,*
> *And every sturdy wall;*
> *The peace of God, the peace of man,*

The peace of love, on all.

CONSECRATION

Laid on Thy altar, my Lord divine
Accept my gift this day for Jesus' sake;
I have no jewels to adorn Thy shrine,
Nor any world-famed sacrifice to make.
But here I bring within my trembling hands
This will of mine—a thing that seemeth small
And only Thou, dear Lord, canst understand
How, when I yield Thee this, I yield mine all.
Hidden therein Thy searching eyes can see
Struggles of passion, visions of delight,
All that I love or am, or fain would be—
Deep loves, fond hope, and longing infinite.
It hath been wet with tears and dimmed with sighs:
Clinched in my grasp till beauty it hath none.
Now, from Thy footstool, where it vanquished lies,
The prayer ascendeth, O, may Thy will be done.
Take it, Oh, Father, ere my courage fail:
And merge it so in Thine own will that e'en
If in some desperate hour my cries prevail
And thou give back my gift, it may have been
So changed, so purified, so fair have grown,
So one with Thee, so filled with peace divine,
I may not know, or feel it as my own,
But gaining back my will, may find it Thine.
                    —AUTHOR UNKNOWN

THE SEED OF LIFE

The fundamental law of the Universe is that every form of life holds *within itself* vitality enough to draw to it every element it needs for growth and fruition. But it is only as it casts off all outside support, and puts its dependence solely upon the life force that created it and left its spark within it, that it is able to draw to itself the elements it needs for complete growth and fruition.

Take the giant redwoods of California. By no law known to man can they draw water to their foliage hundreds of feet in the air! Yet they do draw it—hundreds of gallons every day.

It is not done through pressure from below—from the roots. It is done by pull from above! In other words, the need is first established, then the need itself provides the means or the "pull" to draw to it the elements it must have for expression!

All through Nature, you will find that same law. First the need, then the means. Use what you have to provide the vacuum, then draw upon the necessary elements to fill it. Reach up with your stalk, spread out your branches, provide the "pull" and you can leave to your roots the search for the necessary nourishment. If you have reached high enough, if you have made your magnet strong enough, you can draw to yourself whatever elements you need, no matter if they be at the ends of the earth!

God formed a Seed of Himself in you. He gave it power to attract to itself everything it needs for its growth, just as He did with the seed of the tree. He gave it power to draw to itself everything it needs for fruition, just as He did with the tree. But He did even more for you. He gave your Seed of Life power to attract to itself everything it needs for its *infinite expression!*

You see, Life is intelligent. Life is all-powerful. And Life is always and everywhere seeking expression. What is more, it is never satisfied. It is constantly seeking greater and fuller expression. The moment a tree stops growing, that moment the life in it starts seeking elsewhere for means to better express itself. The moment you stop expressing more and more of Life, that moment Life starts looking around for other and better outlets.

The only thing that can restrict Life is the channel through which it works. The only limitation upon it is the limitation you put upon it.

The secret of success lies in this: There is inside you a Seed of God capable of drawing to you any element you need, to bring to fruition whatever of good you desire. But like all other seeds, its shell must be broken before the kernel inside can use its attractive power. And that shell is thicker, harder, than the shell of any seed on earth. Only one thing will break it—*heat from within*—a desire so strong, a determination so intense, that you cheerfully throw everything you have into the scale to win what you want. Not merely your work and your money and your thought but the willingness to stand or fall by the result—to do or to die. Like the Master when He cursed the fig tree for its barrenness, you are willing to demand of the Seed of Life in you that it *bear fruit or perish.*

That is the secret of every great success. That is the means by which all of life, from the beginning of time, has won what it needed.

What was it gave to certain animals protective shells, to others great speed, to still others a sting, to those who needed them claws or horns? What gave to the bold and strong the means to destroy, to the weak and cowardly facilities for hiding or escape? What but the Seed of Life in each, giving to every form of life the means that form craved to preserve its skin.

Since the very creation of the earth, Life has been threatened by every kind of danger. Had it not been stronger than any other power in the Universe—were it not indeed a part of God Himself—it would have perished ages ago. But God who gave it to us endowed it with unlimited resource, unlimited energy. No other force can defeat it. No obstacle can hold it back.

What is it that saves men in dire extremity, who have exhausted every human resource and finally turned to God in their need? What but the unquenchable flame of God in them—the Seed of Life He has given to each of us—with power to draw to us whatever element we feel that we need to save us from extinction.

The story is told of a little girl four years old, who had been taught to believe in a protecting Deity. She got lost one day, and was gone for hours. Her mother was on the verge of desperation when at last she saw her child coming home. She was all alone, yet seemed to be holding somebody's hand and her lips were moving as if she were carrying on a sprightly conversation. Her mother opened the front door just in time to see her drop the invisible hand and to hear her say:

"You may go now, God. This is where I live. And thank you very much!"

It was all quite simple as she explained it to her mother. She had wandered about until she got tired and hungry. Then she realized that she didn't know the way home.

"I knew I was losted, Mother," she said, "so I asked God to take me home. I knew that He knew the way. Then I started for home and God showed me where to go. And here I am."

"Why, then," some will ask, "does not the God in you exert itself to bring you food when you are hungry, drink when you are thirsty, clothing when you are cold, money when you are in debt?" Why? Because you don't put your dependence upon it for these. You look for these things to your hands or your friends or some means within the power of those around you. It is only when you despair of all ordinary means, it is only *when you convince it* that it must help you or you perish, that the Seed of Life in you bestirs itself to provide a new resource.

That is why psychological or metaphysical means so seldom cure a patient who continues to put some of his dependence upon drugs or treatments. It is not that the spirit in you is a "jealous God." It is that it takes a real need to stir Him into action. As long as you show that you feel there is a chance of your being saved through some other means, the Seed of Life in you is not going to bestir itself to help you. And as long as it sees that you are depending upon your friends or the stock market or some other method to supply your urgent need of money, it is not going to worry itself about it.

"Unity Weekly" tells of a woman alone in a big city, jobless, anxious and discouraged, and worried about her husband who was seeking work in another town.

Because there was no one else to whom she could look for help, she prayed until she was able to put utter faith in God, to believe that He would look after her and to put all her dependence upon Him. Then she was able to go out into the street with springy step, with a heart full of confidence and a face that radiated belief in herself and in her ability to do things. She threw away her sheet of Want Ads, and on impulse, turned into a cheerful looking building and found a desirable job! Within a day or two after, an unexpected check came to her in the mail, and a letter of good news from her husband.

Another case was that of a subnormal boy, about to be rejected by a school. His mother had taught him to believe in God, so he kept repeating to himself—"God will tell me what to do." God did—to such good purpose that a few years later he graduated at the head of his class!

Then there was a woman who was expected to die from a seemingly incurable and painful disease. She asked that her bed be moved to a window, and as she looked out at the starry spaces in the long hours of the night, she thought of God—of His power, of His goodness, of His love for every creature, of Jesus saying that not even a sparrow fell without His marking it. And as she pondered all this, belief in His ability and His willingness to cure her came to her, until presently there began to flow into her consciousness the belief that she WAS cured, and she amazed her attendants by sitting up and asking for something to eat. Today she is alive and well.

How can YOU stir the boundless force of the God in you into action? How can YOU draw upon its infinite resource for your urgent needs?

Utter faith, utter dependence—that is the only answer. No half-way measures will do. If you want help and have exhausted all the methods that physicians and surgeons and practitioners can offer you, and want now to go direct to the Source for new Life, new health and strength, you cannot keep on dabbling with drugs and treatments and hope to stir the Seed of Life in you into action. You must drop everything else. You must put your whole dependence upon the infinite power of that Seed of God in you. You must get the attitude of our revolutionary patriots—"Sink or swim, live or die, survive or perish, I give my hand and my heart to this cause. Either I live by it or I die with it!"

Get that attitude of mind, and the stirring of your Seed of Life into action is simple.

Say to yourself—"I am one with the Life Force that runs the Universe, the great I AM of which Jesus said—'Before Abraham, was I AM.' I AM energy. I AM power. I AM filled with omnipotent life. The vitality of God permeates every fiber of my being. I AM well and whole in every part of my body. I AM made up of billions of cells of Intelligent Life, and that Intelligence is guiding me to Health and Happiness and Prosperity."

E. Stanley Jones, author of CHRIST OF THE INDIAN ROAD, tells how he broke down completely with nervous exhaustion and brain fatigue at the end of eight years of missionary work in India, just when he had learned the ways of the people, and conditions seemed ripe for him to do the most good.

He was terribly depressed and disappointed, until one night in the midst of his prayers, he seemed to hear a voice saying—"Are you yourself ready for this work to which I have called you?" "No, Lord," he answered, "I am done for. I have reached the end of my resources." "If you will turn that over to me," the voice told him, *"and not worry about it,* I will take care of it." "Lord," he responded gladly, "I close the bargain right here!"

That was many years ago. The Doctors had just told him he would have to leave India and go back home for a couple of years to rest. Instead, he threw himself with renewed energy into his work, and he never before knew such health as he has had since. He seems to have tapped a new source of life for body, mind and spirit. *Yet all he had to do was to take it!*

Does this mean that you are to make no effort to help yourself? By no means! This was never meant for a lazy man's world. The whole purpose of existence is growth, and all nature is continually growing. Whenever anything stops growing, it starts to die.

We were given hands to work with, brains to think with. We were expected to use these.

For while it is not the roots that send the moisture to the tops of the tall trees, it is the roots that dig down to the moisture and nutriment to start it flowing. It requires an urgent need to draw to you resources beyond the power of your hands, just as it requires the exaporation of the moisture in the leaves to pull the water to the tops of the tallest trees, but unless the hands or the roots do their part first, that need will never be satisfied. The trouble with most people is that they go as far as their hands or their immediate abilities will take them, and stop there. It is as though a tree sent up its stem only as high as the root pressure carried the water from the earth. That would give us a forest of stunted trees, just as dependence upon their hands gives us the masses who live in poverty and misery.

It is only when you multiply your hands by thousands, it is only when you conceive and start great projects impossible of attainment by you alone, that you call forth the power of the Seed of Life in you, to draw to you every element you need for complete growth and fruition.

When George Mueller of England started his first orphanage, he had no money, no backers, no material resources to depend upon. He saw the need, that is all, so he went as far as he could in supplying that need. And each time, when he had reached the end of his resources, yet kept confidently trying, the need was met! In fifteen years, he built five orphanages and spent more than $5,000,000—all without a single visible means of support!

When St. Theresa proposed to build an orphanage, she was asked how much she had on which to start. When it developed that her total wealth was only three ducats, her superiors laughed at the idea. "It is true," she answered them, "that with only three ducats I can do nothing, but with God and three ducats I can do anything!" And she proceeded to prove it by building the orphanage whose good work made her famous.

In the fields of philanthropy and religion, you can find hundreds of similar stories. And in the fields of business, you find many thousands more. How many times have you read of some great institution that was founded on nothing but hard work and the faith of its founder. Henry Ford began on little else. Stewart started what is now the John Wanamaker store with a total cash capital of $1.50.

Sometimes, in fact, it seems to be an advantage not to have enough money when you start a new project. Then you don't put your faith in the money—you put it in IDEAS. In other words, you look to MIND to supply the means.

Someone expressed it well when he said we must work as if everything depended upon us, and at the same time, pray as if everything depended upon God.

What does an oculist do when you go to him for glasses? Fit your eyes with glasses that take away ALL the strain and enable you to see perfectly? No, indeed! The best oculists give you glasses a little short of the strength necessary to take all the strain off your eyes. They relieve you of the heavy burden, but they leave your sight just enough short of perfection to keep your eyes working towards that end.

The result? When you go back six months or a year later, your eyes are stronger—you can take glasses which do less of your work—until in time you do without them altogether.

What do business leaders advise young people today? Live within your income? No, indeed! *Go into debt!* Reach out! Spread yourself! Then dig the harder to catch up!

You are entitled to just as much of the good things of life as Ford or Rockefeller or Morgan, or any of the rich men around you. But it is not THEY who owe it to you. And it is not the world that owes you a living. The world and they owe you nothing but honest pay for the exact service you render them.

The one who owes you everything of good—riches and honor and happiness—is the God inside you. Go to him! Stir him up! Don't rail against the world. You get from it what you put into it—nothing more. Wake up the God inside you! Demand of him that he bring you the elements you need for riches or success. Demand—and make your need seem as urgent as must have been the need of the crustacean to develop a shell, of the bird to grow wings, of the bear to get fur.

Demand—and KNOW THAT YOU RECEIVE! The God in you is just as strong as ever He was in those primitive animals in pre-historic days. If He could draw from the elements whatever was necessary to give the elephant its trunk, the camel its hump, the bird its wings, and to each creature the means it required to enable it to survive, don't you suppose He can do the same today to provide YOU with the factors you consider essential to your well-being?

The answer is that you have already brought into being your "hump" or your "trunk" or whatever it was that you felt you must have. You are, in short, what your thoughts and fears and beliefs have made you. *Your present condition reflects the successful result of your past thought!*

Astonishing as it may sound to many people, you are now living in a world of your own making. But you don't have to keep on living there if you don't like it. You can build a new world in exactly the same way you built that one—only it would be well to build it on a different model.

It is the Einstein doctrine of the extended line, which must return to its source. An evil thought or act goes out upon its course, but the Eternal Lawmaker has decreed that it must return to its creator. A good act or thought is governed in the same way. "By their fruits, ye shall know them."

So don't complain of your lot. Don't rail at the difficulties and obstacles that confront you. Smile on them! Treat them as friends. *Bless them*—for they can be made to bless you!

You see, they have not been sent from Heaven to punish you. You asked for them yourself. They are of your own making, and they are your friends, because they call forcibly to your attention some wrong method you have been using. All you have to do is to change your methods, and the results will automatically change with them. It is just as though you were doing some problem in multiplication, and you kept saying—"One times one is two." That would throw your whole result out of balance, and it would stay out until you learned your mistake and made one times one equal one.

> *You are not higher than your lowest thought,*
> *Or lower than the peak of your desire.*
> *And all existence has no wonder wrought*
> *To which ambition may not yet aspire.*
> *O Man! There is no planet, sun or star*

Could hold you, if you but knew what you are.

What, then, is the method to be used to get what you want from life?

1st—DESIRE. Decide what it is you want. Make it something so worthwhile that all other things will seem small and unimportant beside it, something so urgent that you can say to the God Inside You—*"Give me this or I perish!"*

2nd—See *yourself having it.* Visualize the thing you want. See yourself with it. Try to get the FEEL of having it, the joy and thankfulness you would get out of it. In Burton Rascoe's Memoirs, he tells how he worked out his life on a predetermined schedule, in which everything came true because he thought it, he desired it and he BELIEVED it. Here are a few typical lines from it:

When I was fifteen years old, I wanted to live in Chicago some time and I *knew* I would; the university I wished to go to was the University of Chicago and I *knew* I would; there was only one newspaper in the world I ardently wished to work on—the "Chicago Tribune"—and I *knew* five years in advance that I would some day work there; when I was a reporter I *knew* I would be some day literary editor.

When I was literary editor of the "Chicago Tribune" I *knew* I would some day live in New York and be literary editor of the "New York Tribune".

In 1927 I wanted $50,000 and *knew* I would get it; within less than a year I had over $100,000, almost without any effort on my part.

3rd—*Be thankful for having received it.* Remember the admonition of the Master—"Whatsoever things ye ask for when ye pray, believe that ye RECEIVE them, and ye shall have them." You cannot believe that you actually receive the things you ask for without being thankful for them. So give thanks, sincere thanks, for having received the things you prayed for, and try to FEEL grateful. Remember to SMILE! Repeat aloud daily Adelaide Proctor's poem—

My God, I thank Thee, who has made the earth so bright;
So full of splendor and of joy, beauty and light;
So many glorious things are here, noble and right.

I thank Thee too that Thou hast made joy to abound;
So many gentle thoughts and deeds circling us round,
That in the darkest spot of earth Thy love is found.

4th—*Act as though you HAD already received* the thing you asked for. Faith without works is dead. Do some physical thing each day such as you would do if you had the object you prayed for. If you are asking for money, for instance, GIVE a little, even though it be only a dime, just to show the freedom from money worry that is now yours. If you are asking for love, say a kindly word to each of those with whom you come in contact. If you are asking for health, dance about your room, sing, laugh, do some of those things you will do when you have fully manifested the good health you crave.

5th—*Show your affection* for the thing you asked for. Give your love to it, pour it out just as you would if you had the object in your hands. Only by making it REAL to you in your thoughts can you materialize it in your life.

We go, you know, in the direction of our thoughts. What we long for—*and expect*—that we are headed towards. So look for the kind of things you want to see. Look for them in your own life—and in the lives of those around you. Look for them—AND BEGIN DOING THEM! Remember those lines of Goethe's:

Are you in earnest? Seize this very minute;
What you can do, or dream you can, begin it;
Boldness has genius, power, and magic in it.
Only engage, and then the mind grows heated;
Begin, and then the work will be completed.

AFTER ITS KIND

Do you know what is the most important lesson in the whole Bible? Do you know what principle was considered so vital that God is said to have used it on three of the six days of creation, and it is repeated no less than six times in the first chapter of Genesis alone? Just this:

"Everything Reproduces After Its Kind!"

Go back over the miracles of increase in the Bible. What do you find? When the widow of Zarephath gave Elijah her oil and meal, what did she get? MORE OIL AND MEAL, did she not? Not gold, or riches, but INCREASE AFTER ITS KIND.

When another widow begged Elisha to save her sons from bondage, he asked—"What hast thou in the house?" And when told—"Naught save a pot of oil," it was the *oil* he increased, was it not?

When the multitude lacked for bread and the Apostles asked Jesus what they should do, He did not turn the stones into bread, or bring forth gold with which to buy. No, He asked—"How many loaves have you?" And when told five, and two fishes, He based His increase upon *them.*

You see, it all comes back to terms of electrical energy, for what is energy but power, and what are personality, skill, ability, riches, but different forms of power? If you want to increase your stock of these, what must you do? Put them to work, must you not? Put them out at interest, as in the parable of the talents. No energy ever expanded until it was released. No seed ever multiplied until it was sown. No talent ever increased until it was used.

You want more power, more riches, greater ability, a wider field of usefulness. How are you going to get them? *Only by putting out at interest that which you have!*

And the way to do this lies—NOT in working for riches as such—BUT FOR INCREASE IN THE FORM OF ENERGY YOU HAVE!

Now, what have YOU in the house? What seed can you plant, what service can you give?

In "Weekly Unity" some years ago, there was the story of a mother who had been well-to-do, but had lost everything and was now hard put to it to provide food and clothing for her small boys. It was near Christmas, and she was bewailing to a friend the fact that she could buy no gifts for her children, much less remember old friends and relatives.

The friend smiled. "Money is not what you need," she told her. "Can money buy the gifts that live in your heart? If I were in your place, I should stop repining and, instead, seek the guidance of your Inner Self."

The mother took the advice, and one night, as she dropped off to sleep after having prayed for guidance, she saw a beautiful tree, lighted with tapers, and beneath each light hung a small envelope. As she looked more closely, she saw that the names written on the envelopes were those of friends and relatives to whom she longed to give.

Opening one of the envelopes, she found a piece of blank paper and she seemed to hear a voice saying: "Write, and let that which you write bear witness of Me. As you write, give from your heart the treasures that are stored there in My name. I will fulfill every blessing according to your word."

The mother woke, and going immediately to her desk, began to write her blessings. She wrote words of life and wholeness for an aunt who had been bound with rheumatism for months; words of courage for an uncle who was having a difficult time with his farm; words of guidance for a young cousin who had seemed to lose her way a bit. Inspired by that Inner Self, she wrote ten blessings that night.

She had never thought that she could write, but her own heart thrilled at the beauty of the words that came to her, and she was lifted up by their power and simplicity. "Don't ever again say you have nothing to give," one of her friends told her later. "I never received so richly in all my life." And throughout the years, the blessings that this mother gave out have continued to bear fruit.

"Give me gold," prayed Levesco, "that I may be helpful, not helpless. Give me gold that I may taste the pure joy of making others happy. Give me gold that I may see the beauties of this world in moments of leisure. Give me gold that I and mine may be secure in our declining years."

A worthy prayer, indeed. But prayer alone is not enough. You must plant the seed before you can hope to reap the harvest. You must give before you can get.

"DO THE THING," said Emerson, "and you shall have the power. But they who do *not* the thing, have not the power. Everything has its price, and if the price is not paid— not that thing but something else is obtained. And it is impossible to get anything without its price.

"For any benefit received a tax is levied. In nature nothing can be given—all things are sold.

"Power to him who power exerts."

Russell Conwell, the famous lecturer, who built the Baptist Temple in Philadelphia and founded Temple University, was in the beginning merely the pastor of a very poor flock. His congregation consisted of working people, and many of them were in need. So he was continually offering prayers for money.

One Sunday, it occurred to him that the old Jewish custom had been to make a gift or offering first, and then pray for what you wanted. So he announced that the following Sunday, he would reverse his usual method of procedure. Instead of offering his prayer first, he would first take up the collection, and he wanted all who had special favors to ask of God to give freely as an "Offering." We quote the result from "Effective Prayer":

The question was asked afterward if anyone who made a special offering on that particular day had not been answered, and there was no exception in the mass of testimony to the efficiency of each prayer that day. The recitals of the marvels which followed that prayerful offering were too startling for general belief. The people had complied with the conditions, and God had answered clearly according to His promise. They had brought the tithes into the storehouse, and the Lord had poured out the blessings as an infallible result.

Cases of sudden and instaneous recovery of the sick were related by hundreds. One poor man whose child was insane prayed for her recovery. That afternoon when he went to the sanitarium, she met him in her right mind.

A lady sold her jewelry and brought the proceeds as an offering as she prayed for healing from sciatic rheumatism. She fell going from the Church, and arose to find the rheumatism gone.

One old gentleman involved in a ruinous lawsuit brought all the profits of the previous week and deposited them as he prayed for a just outcome. Within the week, the suit was withdrawn.

A woman with an overdue mortgage on her home determined to risk all on one prayer, and gave all she had as she prayed. When plumbers came to repair a leak the following week, they discovered a loose board in the floor under which her father had hidden all his money. The sum was more than enough to pay off the mortgage in its entirety.

There were probably fifty such cases.

You have to sow before you can reap. You have to give before you can get. And when you sow, when you give, you must give freely with no strings to it. As Jesus put it— "Except a kernel of wheat fall into the ground and die, it abideth alone. But if it die, it beareth much fruit."

You remember the old-fashioned hand-pumps that are still to be found on many farms. To start them, you had to pour in a bucket of water, in order to create a vacuum and thus be able to draw water from the well. The same principle applies in using a siphon. You pour in water to drive out the air and create a vacuum. Once the vacuum is formed, your water flows, and you can get unlimited quantities of it without having to give more. But you get none from pump or siphon until you first give some.

You must give to get. You must sow the seed you have before you can reap the harvest. You cannot merely lend it. You must GIVE it, freely and fully. "Except a kernel of wheat fall into the ground and DIE," said the Master. Except your seed of riches be given freely and fully, you get nothing from it. "But if it die, it beareth much fruit." If it be dead to you—if it is gone beyond hope of return, then you can look for a harvest.

"He that findeth his life shall lose it," said the Master on another occasion, "but he that loseth his life for My sake shall find it." He that gives all he has in the service of his fellows shall find that in so doing, he has planted seeds which will bring him a harvest of happiness and plenty.

You have probably read the story of Charles Page, as given in the "American Magazine" a few years ago. Page was then a millionaire oil operator in Oklahoma, but a few years before he had little or nothing, and his wife was so sick he feared he was going to lose her as well. The surgeons at the hospital had given up hope for her, so as all other avenues seemed closed, Page turned to God.

"Oh, Lord," he prayed, "don't take her away from me. I just couldn't bear it."

The words rang in his ears—and they had an empty ring. As a prayer, it seemed to fall flat. Why should the Lord interfere for him, if the only reason he could offer was that he couldn't bear it? Plenty of husbands just as devoted as he had lost their wives. Why should the Lord specially favor him?

The thought came home to him with the power of a blow. What had he ever done that the Lord should go out of His way to help him? What reason had he to look for special consideration from above? None! He'd been a decent enough citizen, but no more so than the average, and kneeling there he couldn't recall a single thing he had done which would entitle him to ask favors from the Lord.

The thought appalled him. What chance had he? Must he then lose the one dearest to him in all the world, just because he had never done enough to be worthy of keeping her? No! No! That was unthinkable. It wasn't too late. He would start that very minute. What was it the Master had said? "Whatsoever ye do unto the least of these My brethren, ye do it unto Me."

The next morning a poor widow was in transports of joy to find under her doorsill money enough to carry her safely through the winter.

But that evening inquiry at the hospital elicited the information that Page's wife was no better. For a little his faith faltered. Then, as he thought back over the reason for his act, it flamed up anew. Why had he helped the widow? Not because he was interested in her welfare, not even because it was the right thing to do, but because he was trying to buy off the Lord. Thinking of it in that light, it sounded ridiculous. He got down on his knees again.

"I ain't makin' a bargain with You, God," he promised. "I'm doin' this because it's the *right thing* for me to do."

This time it seemed to him his message carried. He felt strangely cheered and relieved. His prayer had gone through.

Now comes the remarkable part of this incident. His wife, much to the astonishment of the surgeons, took a turn for the better, and within a comparatively short time was well!

From that day to this Charles Page has never failed in his Covenant with God. Times there were when everything looked black. Times when it meant a real struggle to find the Lord's share. But his faith never faltered. He knew if he did his part, he could depend upon God for His.

For a long time, he gave a tenth of all his earnings. Then he increased it to a fourth. Later to a half, and finally to all except what he needed for personal and family expenses. He has given away literally millions.

"But don't get the idea," he warns, "that I'm telling you how to get rich. It's the *giving*, not the *getting*, that is important. Personally, I believe that it's only playing fair to tithe, or give a part of your income to God. But it must be a gift, not an investment. Do you get the difference? If you tithe in the right spirit, you will get your reward just as sure as a gun's iron; but the reward may not come in the form of money. Often it's something far better than money . . ."

"What you keep to yourself you lose," wrote Munthe. "What you give away, you keep forever." And Irene Stanley expressed much the same thought in her little poem—

> *You have to let go of the rung below*
> *When you reach for the round above.*
> *There is no other way to climb, you know,*
> *You have to let go of the rung below.*
> *Each upward step brings more of the glow*
> *And warmth of the Sun of hove,*
> *You have to let go of the rung below,*
> *When you reach for the round above.*

You see, God incarnates Himself through you. But He cannot be shut up. He must be given out, expressed. You put Him into everything you do, whether towards failure or success. You are inseparable from the creative force. You are part of the fountain head of supply.

What then must you do to win riches and success? GIVE! Give freely of what you have.

> Give, and it shall be given unto you; good measure, pressed down, and shaken together, and running over, shall men give unto your bosom. For with the same measure that ye mete withal it shall be measured to you again.
>
> –LUKE 6:38.

Does that require too great faith? You do not marvel at the farmer who freely throws all his seed into the ground, knowing he will never see it again, but must depend upon its fruit for his increase. He shows perfect faith. Should you show less?

Remember the first Law of Life, the law that was considered so important that it was repeated six times in the first Chapter of Genesis: *"Everything increases after its kind."*

Do you expect that law to be changed for you? Do you expect to reap without sowing? "There is that scattereth and increaseth yet more," said that wisest of ancient sages, King Solomon. "And there is that withholdeth more than is meet, *but it tendeth to poverty.*

"The liberal soul shall be made fat, and he that watereth, shall be watered himself."

You see, Life is logical. Life follows definite, fundamental laws. One of these laws is that you reap as you sow, that "He that hath a bountiful eye shall be blessed."

For all motion is cyclic. It circulates to the limit of its possibilities and then returns to its starting point. Thus any unselfish expenditure of energy returns to you laden with gifts. Any unselfish act done for another's benefit is giving part of yourself. It is an outward flow of power that completes its cycle and returns laden with energy.

Everything we get, we pay for—good or bad. Personal gain comes through impersonal service. Personal loss comes through selfishness.

As Emerson puts it—"A perfect equity adjusts its balance in all parts of life. *Every act rewards itself."* Any act of ours that injures another, separates us from God. Any act of ours that helps others, brings us closer to God and Good. One may think that his cheating of another is a secret between them, but by his cheating, he has shaken the trust of another in human brotherhood and damaged his idealism. Isn't that a definite affront that is going to stand between him and God when the one who cheated tries to enlist God's help in enlarging the activities of his own life?

Wouldn't it have been better to say to himself: "God gives me all my money. Surely He has given me enough for all the needs of my business, or if He hasn't already given it, it is on the way. If I need more, He will give me more. So I am not even going to think about trying to make 'easy money' by taking advantage of others. God provides me with plenty, and I am going to run this business as if He were always here beside me."

One on God's side is a majority. You are always together with God. So make Him an active partner in your business. Look to Him for its needs, give the same loving service you feel that He would give. Then cast off all worries fears, and *put your business lovingly in His hands.* When the future looks dark, when problems confront you, just say to yourself:

> *God lights the way; no more I grope,*
> *Nor stumble on in troubled hope.*
> *I sow no seeds of care and strife;*
> *But those of love, and joy, and life.*
> *No more I strive to plan my lot;*
> *The Father fills my cup unsought.*

What is the Unpardonable Sin? What but damming the sources of God's supply. What but trying to shut up the God in you, trying to keep Him from expressing Himself.

When the giant monsters of antiquity ceased developing, and depended upon their size and strength and fierceness, they perished. When the vast Empires of China and Greece and Persia and Rome stopped reaching out and tried merely to hold what they had, they died. When the rich man or big business of today stops giving service and merely hangs on to his fortune, he loses it.

You cannot stand still. You must go forward—or die.

There is a God in you seeking expression. You cannot keep Him shut up. You must give Him channels through which to express Himself, or He will rend you and come out of you.

What would you think of a man who spent years in developing great muscles, then tried to keep them great by not using them, by not wearing them out? You'd call him a fool, wouldn't you, because everyone knows that the only way to develop muscles is to use them, the only way to keep them strong is to continually exercise them.

What everyone does not seem to know is that all of life works in the same way. You cannot hold on to anything good. You must be continually giving—and getting. You cannot hold on to your seed. You must sow it—and reap anew. You cannot hold on to riches. You must use them and get other riches in return.

The Unpardonable Sin is to stand in the way of progress, try to stop the cycle of life.

You must give to get. You must sow to reap. The unprofitable servant in Jesus' parable was not the first or the only one to be cast into outer darkness where is weeping and gnashing of teeth, from burying his talent. The ones who became rulers over many things were those who freely used what they had—who started riches *flowing!*

So when a "talent" is given you, don't try to hide it away or bury it. Don't dam up the channels of supply with the few dollars you have, and thus prevent the unlimited riches of God from flowing to you.

Set up your generator, which is the service you have to offer your fellowman. Turn on the steam by giving to it all the power, all the skill, all the intelligence you have. Then start the flow of riches with your faith by cheerfully pouring into the channel of service all that you have. That means buy the things that are necessary to your development and that of your family. Pay your just debts, though it leaves you without a cent in your purse. Put your dependence—NOT on the few dollars you have in hand, but on the great ocean of supply above and about you. Use the few dollars you have to create the vacuum which shall poke a hole in the bottom of that ocean, and start the unending flow of riches pouring into you.

You remember that Jesus once likened the power of God to the leaven in bread. You put a tiny yeast cake into a great pan of dough and it affects the whole mixture. It makes it GROW. Apparently it INCREASES the quantity of flour, milk, eggs and other ingredients—certainly it makes them bulk to several times their original size.

That yeast is the "God in you" that you put into your circumstances, your affairs. Put it into fears and worries, and it will increase them until they can hardly be borne. Put it into your expenses, and it will make them ever greater. Put it into love and life and good work, and it will bring these back to you increased a hundredfold.

"Let's have a league of optimists," writes Elizabeth Swaller in LET'S HAVE IT,

> *To boost the world along.*
> *We are so weary of the thought*
> *That everything is wrong!*
>
> *We're surfeited with talk of lack,*
> *Depression, gloom and fear.*
> *If we but think of brighter things,*
> *Good times will soon be here.*
>
> *'Tis time to turn and face about*
> *And court conditions fine.*
> *By boosting, I shall prosper yours,*
> *And you will prosper mine.*

Put your yeast into optimistic thoughts, into kindly words, into loving acts of service. Remember, the hardest part of anything is the start. If you want something, pray for it—then START doing, being, giving—whatever is needful to set the yeast acting. You don't have to make the dough expand when you put the yeast into it. The yeast attends to that. All you have to do is to give the yeast a chance to get in its work!

So if you want to receive something of good, show your faith by GIVING of what you have. Put a little yeast into your affairs. It doesn't matter how poor you are, how much in debt, how weak or sickly. You can always give something. But remember that everything increases after its kind, so give of what you want to receive. Sow the seeds of the harvest you want to reap, whether it be love, energy, service or money.

And PRAY! Nearly 2,000 years before Christ, it was said in the Vedas that if two people would unite their psychic forces, they could conquer the world. Then came Jesus, to put it even more definitely: "Again I say unto you, that if two of you shall agree on earth as touching anything that they shall ask, it shall be done for them of my Father which is in Heaven. For when two or three are gathered together in my name, there am I in the midst of them."

In one of his books, Russell Conwell tells of a little group in his church who were in such straitened circumstances that they decided to get together and see if, by uniting their prayers, they could not improve their finances.

So they met at the house of one of their number who happened to be a bookbinder by trade, and decided that each week the whole group would unite their prayers to solve the difficulties of some one member.

The bookbinder was the first one chosen. He owed a great deal of money, and had no means of paying his debts. So that evening, the group prayed that he might receive help in meeting his obligations. It was then agreed that at noontime every day until the next meeting, each member would stop whatever he was doing, and spend a minute or two in silent prayer that the bookbinder's needs might be met.

The meeting was on Tuesday evening. The next day after lunch, as was his custom, the bookbinder dropped into a publishing house nearby for a chat with some friends. He met there a man from Washington who told him that "for the first time in his life, he had forgotten his train," and must now get back home on some urgent business, without placing a contract which he had intended to give to a New York bookbinder.

The bookbinder suggested that he also was in that business, and possibly could help him, but the other objected that the particular class of work he wanted could be done only in New York. Upon the binder persisting, however, he explained his needs, and being convinced that they could be filled right there in as satisfactory a way and on more reasonable terms than in New York, he not only gave the binder the contract, *but advanced enough money to more than take care of his difficulties!*

The binder hurried to the other members of his group and told them of his good fortune. His problem was so completely solved that he felt they ought to start work at once for some other member, because all were so badly in need. All felt so elated over their success in helping the binder solve his problem, that they chose the most difficult case of all as the next.

This was a jeweler who had grown so old and forgetful that his business was in a deplorable condition. Bankruptcy seemed so sure that his son had moved out of town to avoid sharing the disgrace.

Two or three days after the group started working on the jeweler's problem, the son came to town for a day to attend a funeral. On the return trip from the cemetery, he fell into conversation with one of the other mourners, in the course of which the latter mentioned that he was looking for an expert in clock making to superintend a new factory he was erecting in another city.

The son told him his father was a master of that art, but no good at managing finances. The upshot of it was that the jeweler applied for the position, at the same time explaining his present financial difficulties. The manufacturer liked his letter, went over the whole situation with him, and ended by taking over the store as a retail outlet, paying off the old debts, and forming a business connection with the jeweler which prospered both amazingly.

An old lady who owned a small notion store was next. Soon after the group united in prayer for her, a fire destroyed the store next door to her. The owner decided to build bigger than before, and offered her not only an attractive price for her store, but an interest in his business, which paid her enough to live in comfort the rest of her days.

Every Member of that Group Became Prosperous!

Do you, too, want something very much? Then give— *and pray!* Get yourself a small toy bank—a paper one will do. Each day put something into it, even though it be only a penny. Give that money to God. Give it to Him at the time you put it into the bank, but leave it there until it

amounts to a dollar or more. Then use it for any good charitable purpose that presents itself.

Don't give it to some panhandler. Try to use it where it will do the
recipient some good. Use it to help him to help himself, as in buying
some book for him that will show him the way out of his difficulties.

And as you give, *pray!* Pray not only for yourself, but for others.

Every morning at seven, we shall pray for protection for our own
family, and for all students of this Course who will join with us in
"uniting their psychic forces" by "agreeing as to the thing they should
ask." For this prayer, you cannot do better than repeat the ninety-first
Psalm.

Every day at noon, we shall pray for abundant supply for all of those
among our readers who will join with us in praying for the whole group.
For this prayer, hold in your hand any money you intend to give that
day for any good purpose, and any checks or money you intend to use
to pay bills, and say with us:

I bless you . . . and be thou a blessing. May you enrich all who touch
you. I thank God for you, but even more I thank Him that there are
billions like you where you came from. I bless that Infinite Supply. I
thank God for it and I expand my consciousness to take it in. (Here try
to see in your mind's eye a Niagara of money flowing to you and to all
who are praying with you. See yourself and all of us bringing in a great
net full of money like the nets the Apostles pulled in bursting with fish.)
I release that Infinite Supply through all my channels and the channels
of all the students of this Course just as I freely release the money I hold
in my hand, giving it where it will do the most good. The Spirit that
multiplied the loaves and fishes for Jesus enters into this money, making
it grow and increase and bring forth fruit an hundredfold. All of God's
channels are now open and flowing for us. The best in ourselves for the
world—the best in the world for us.

Then PREPARE for prosperity. When the Israelites of old were
suffering from drought, and begged the Prophet Elisha to help them,
what was the first thing he told them to do? Fill the valley with
ditches—prepare to RECEIVE the water that they asked for!

You see prayers and affirmations are not for the purpose of
influencing God. He has already done His part. All of good is always

available to each of us. Our prayers and affirmations are for the purpose of bringing our own minds to the point where we can ACCEPT God's gifts! We don't need to work on conditions—we need only to work on ourselves. The only place we can cure our lacks and our troubles *is in our own minds!* When we have done it there, we shall find that they are cured everywhere.

"Whatsoever things ye ask for when ye pray," the Master assured us, "believe that ye HAVE RECEIVED them, and ye shall HAVE them."

That is the basis of all successful prayer, whether for the healing of our bodies, or for material benefits. Once you convince your Higher Self, which is the God in you, that you HAVE the thing you want, *it will proceed immediately to bring it into being!*

But how, you may ask, can I convince my Higher Self that I have riches or any other good thing, when my common sense tells me that I am in debt up to my ears and creditors are hounding me day and night?

You can't—if you keep thinking and acting DEBTS. But here is a psychological fact: The Higher Self accepts as fact anything that is repeated to it in convincing tones often enough. And once it has accepted any statement as fact, it proceeds to do everything possible to MAKE IT TRUE!

That is the whole purpose of affirmations—to bring the God in You to accept as true the conditions that you desire, to the end that He will then proceed to bring them into being. It is a sort of auto-suggestion. You keep saying to yourself that you ARE rich, that you HAVE the things you desire, until the constant repetition is accepted by the Higher Self and translated into its physical equivalent.

Debts? Don't worry about them. Remember that the shadow of growing grain kills the weeds. Keep your mind on the good you want and it will kill off the evil you fear, just as the turning on of light dispels darkness. A farmer does not have to hoe the weeds out of growing wheat, any more than you have to sweep the darkness out of a room. Neither do you have to worry about debts or lack. Put all your thoughts and all your faith in the riches you are praying for, and let them dispel the debts.

But don't worry if you can't summon such faith right out of the blue. Most of us have to lead up to it gradually. Start with Coué's well-known affirmation—"Every day in every way we are getting richer and richer." Use that to prepare your Higher Self for the stronger affirmations. Then, when your faith has grown stronger, *claim the thing you want!* Affirm that you HAVE it—and insofar as possible, ACT AS THOUGH YOU HAD IT!

Write it in your heart that each day is the best day of the year, that NOW is the accepted time, NOW is the day of salvation. Then thank God for the good you have been praying for, believe that you HAVE received and give thanks.

Remember this: God's will always works when you offer no resistance to it. So pray—and then LET His good come to you. Don't fight the conditions about you. Don't try to overcome the obstacles in your path. BLESS them—know that God is in them—that if you will LET them, they will work WITH you for good. Have faith not only in God, but in people and things. Don't look for a miracle to happen. Don't expect an angel from Heaven to come and open the way. Know that God works through ordinary people and things, and it is through them that your good will come.

So bless THEM. Serve them as you would the Lord, doing each thing that is given you to do as though you were the greatest genius. And all day long, as the thought occurs to you, keep repeating to yourself—"Every day in every way I am getting richer and richer," or whatever it is that you desire.

There is something about praying for *others* that oftentimes does one more good than praying for oneself. You see, you cannot give anything to others without first possessing it yourself. When you wish another evil, you draw that evil to yourself first and you usually get a part of it. When you bring good to another, you bring it through yourself, and you share in it.

Remember the experience of Job in the olden days. Despite his lamentations and prayers, he lost all his riches, and his afflictions remained with him. But then misfortune fell upon his friends as well, and in his sympathy for them, Job forgot his own ailments and prayed for his friends. And it is written that—"The Lord turned the captivity of Job, *when he prayed for his friends.* And the Lord gave him twice as much as he had before."

For who upon the hearth can start a fire,
And never warm the stone?
Or who can cheer another's heart,
And not his own?
I stilled a hungry infant's cry,
With kindness filled a stranger's cup,
And lifting others,
Found that I was lifted up!

HOW TO DEVELOP FAITH POWER FOR SUCCESSFUL LIVING

To you, faith has doubtless been a term properly applied in sermons and theological books, but which has but little or no practical place or meaning in the world of action and deeds—in the world in which most of us live most of our time, and perform most of our actions.

We assure you that Faith Power is something having a most intimate and important relation to Personal Power along practical lines, and is something which, in the current phrase, "you need in your business."

Mr. Leon Jolson, president of the huge Necchi Sewing Machine Company, is today worth many millions of dollars. A few years ago he was a poor Polish immigrant who couldn't even speak English. The newspaper account of his spectacular rise to success quoted him as saying, "I had unfaltering faith. I prayed for guidance every step of the way. I used head and foot work."

The general conception of Faith—the idea of Faith held by most persons—is that it is an emotional state independent of, if not indeed actually contrary to Reason. However, we believe that the most important reasoning of practical everyday life is based on Faith. We do not know positively that the sun will rise tomorrow morning—all that we know is that in the history of the race the sun always has risen in the morning, and we "believe" that it will continue the practice on the morrow; but we do not "know" absolutely that such will be the case, we cannot prove it absolutely by argument—even by mathematics—unless we admit the existence of Universal Law, or the law of Causation, whereby "the same causes, under the same conditions will produce the same effects."

You may object to all this as silly—but, instead, it is the strictest application of the rules and laws of practical thought. Of course, you say that we "know" that the sun will rise tomorrow morning, and may even tell to a second the time of its rising. Certainly we "know" this—but we know it only by an act of Faith. That Faith, moreover, is the belief that there exists Universal Law—that "natural things act and move under

Law"—that "the same causes, under the same conditions, produce the same results."

In the ordinary affairs of life and action you act according to Faith. You do this so naturally and instinctively, so constantly and habitually, that you are not aware of it. You start on an airline flight. You buy your ticket, having faith that the plane will start from the airport named on the ticket, and approximately on the time noted in it. You have faith that it will proceed to the destination promised. You do not "know" these things from actual experience—for you cannot so know what lies in the future: you take them for granted, you assume them to be true, you act upon Faith.

You take your seat. You do not know the pilot or the co-pilot—you have never seen them, nor do you even know their names. You do not know whether or not they are competent, reliable, or experienced. All that you know is that it is reasonable to suppose that the plane company will select the right kind of men for the task—you act upon Faith, upon Faith rationally interpreted. You have Faith in the company, in the management, in the system of flights, in the equipment, etc. and you stake your life and wholeness of body upon that Faith. You may say that you only "take a chance" in the matter; but, even so, you manifest Faith in that "chance," or else you wouldn't take it. You wouldn't "take a chance" of standing in the path of a rushing express train, or of leaping from the Empire State Building, would you? You manifest Faith in something—even if that something be no more than the Law of Averages.

You place your money in a bank; here again you manifest Faith—Faith rationally interpreted. You sell goods on credit to your customers—Faith again. You have Faith in your grocer, your butcher, your lawyer, your physician, your clerks, your insurance company. That is to say Faith of some kind, or of some degree—else you would not trust anything whatsoever to them. If you "believe" that a man is dishonest, incompetent, or insane, you do not place confidence in him, nor trust your affairs or interests to him; your Faith is in his "wrongness," and not in his "rightness"—but it is Faith, nevertheless. Every "belief" short of actual, positive knowledge, is a form or phase of Faith.

You have the Faith that if you step off a high building into space, you will fall and be injured, perhaps killed: this is your Faith in the Law of Gravitation. You have a similar Faith in certain other physical laws—you have the Confident Expectation that evil results to you will follow certain courses of action concerning these physical laws. You have Faith that poisons will injure or destroy your physical body, and you avoid such. You may object that you "know" these things, not merely "believe" them; but you don't "know" anything directly and immediately until you experience it—and you cannot experience it—and you cannot experience a future happening before its time. All that you can do concerning each and every future experience is to "believe" certain things concerning it—and that "belief" is nothing else but Faith, interpreted more or less rationally and correctly.

You do not "know" certainly and positively, by direct experience, or by pure reason, a single thing about the happenings of tomorrow, or of some day next week, or of the corresponding day of next year. Yet you act as if you did possess such knowledge—but why? Simply because of your Faith in the Law and Order of the Universe; of the operation of the Law of Causation; whereby effects follow causes; of the law of Probabilities, or of the Law of Average; or of some other Natural Law. But your knowledge of and belief in such Laws are but forms of your Faith, i.e., Confident Expectation that "things will work out according to the rule observed in past actions." You cannot get away from Faith in your thoughts and beliefs concerning the present and the future, any more than you can run away from your shadow in the bright daylight.

From the foregoing, and the reflections aroused in your mind by the consideration of it, you will perceive that Faith has as true and as sound position and place in the psychology of the human being as have Reason and Intellect.

Without the Confident Expectation of Faith, there will be no kindling of the flame of Insistent Desire—no application of the steel of Persistent Determination. Unless Faith expresses itself in the Confident Expectation of the obtaining or attainment of the thing desired and willed, then will Desire find it difficult to "want it hard enough," and Will will find it impossible to "persistently determine to obtain it."

Desire and Will depend upon Faith for their Inspirational Forces—by means of the latter, the Energizing Forces of Desire and the Dynamic Forces of Will are inspired and vitalized, and have the Breath of Life breathed into them.

HOW SICKNESS IS CURED BY FAITH

Among the many phases and forms of the application and manifestation of the mental principle of Faith Power is that important phase or form known generally as "Faith-Cure."

Faith-Cure is a term applied to the practice of curing disease by an appeal to the hope, belief, or expectation of the patient, and without the use of drugs or other material means. Formerly, Faith-Cure was confined to methods requiring the exercise of religious faith, such as the "prayer cure" and "divine healing," but has now come to be used in the broader sense, and includes the cures of Mental Science.

It is now generally agreed that the cures made by the various practitioners of the numerous schools and forms of Faith-Cure have as their underlying effective principle the mental condition or state of Faith; this principle operating so as to call forth the innate power of the mental-physical organism to resist and to overcome the abnormal conditions which manifest as disease. Thus, all cures wrought by the mental forces of the individual, under whatever name or method, are, at the last, Faith-Cures.

This innate power of the organism so lodged in the subconscious mentality, is found to respond readily to the ideas accepted as true by the individual—to his "beliefs," in short. These beliefs are forms of Faith, at the last.

From the psychological point of view, all these different kinds of faith-healing, as indeed all kinds of faith-healing, as indeed all kinds of mind-cure, depend upon suggestion. In faith-healing proper not only are powerful direct suggestions used, but the religious atmosphere and the autosuggestions of the patient co-operate, especially when the cures take place during a period of religious revival or at other times when large assemblies and strong emotions are found. The suggestibility of large crowds is markedly greater than that of individuals, and to this greater faith must be attributed the greater success of the fashionable places of pilgrimage.

Analyzing the phenomena attributed to Suggestion, and reducing the idea of Suggestion to its essential elements, we find that Suggestions consists of: (1) placing a strong idea in the mind—grafting it on the mind, as it were; (2) arousing the Expectant Attention of the results implied or indicated in the suggested idea; and (3) setting into operation the activities of the subconscious mentality in the direction of bringing about the result pictured by the Expectant Attention, which in turn has been aroused by the suggested idea. There you have the whole idea of Suggestion in a nutshell!

Now then, all phenomena of Faith-Cure, and of Suggestion as well, are seen to depend upon the presence and action of the element or principle of Faith Power in the mentality of the individual.

By an application of the first of the above stated elements of this greater principle of your being, and of Nature as a whole, you may keep yourself in health, strength and general desirable physical well-being; or you may bring about by it a gradual return to health and physical well-being if you have lost these; again, if you allow this principle to be directed wrongly and abnormally, you may lose your physical well-being and health, and may start on the downward path of disease, the end of which is an untimely death. Your physical condition is very largely dependent upon the character and kind of the Ideas and Ideals which you permit to be planted in your mind and by the degree of Expectant Attention, or Faith, which you permit to vitalize these Ideas and Ideals.

Briefly stated, the course to be followed by you in this matter is as follows: (1) Encourage Ideas and Ideals of Health, Strength, and Vitality—the ideas of Physical Well-Being—to take lodgment in your mind, there to send forth their roots sprouts, blossoms and fruit; cultivate these Ideas and Ideals and vitalize them with a goodly amount of Expectant Attention, Confident Expectation and Faith along the lines of these conditions which you desire to be present in yourself; see yourself "in your mind's eye" as you wish to be, and "confidently expect" to have these conditions manifested in you by your subconscious mentality; (2) never allow yourself to hold the ideas of diseased abnormal conditions, and, above all, never allow yourself to cultivate the mental habit of "expecting" such conditions to manifest in your body—cultivate the attitude of Faith and Hope, and discard that of Fear; (3) if your mind has been filled with these negative, harmful and destructive mental Ideas and Expectancy, and if your body has manifested Disease in response to them, you should proceed to "kill out" these noxious mental weeds by a deliberate, determined and confident cultivation of the right kind of Ideas and Ideals and states of "Expectancy"; it is an axiom of advanced psychology that "the positives tend to inhibit and to destroy the negatives"—the weeds in the mental garden may be "killed out" by the careful and determined cultivation of the positive plants of Hope, Faith and Confident Expectation of the Good and Desirable.

Faith Power is present and active—it is potent and powerful—and it is friendly to you if you recognize and realize its existence; it is ready to serve you, and to serve you well, provided that you call upon it properly and furnish it with the proper channels through which to flow in its efforts to manifest itself. This is the great truth back of the special lesson of Faith-Cure!

THE MIGHTY SUBCONSCIOUS MIND

The Subconscious—that great field or plane of mental activity—is the seat of far greater power, and the source of far deeper and broader streams of mental force, than the average person even begins to realize. In that field, or on that plane, are performed over seventy-five percent of man's mental activities.

Our mental world is far more extensive than we usually conceive it to be; it has great comparatively unsounded depths, and equally grand comparatively unsealed heights. The explored and charted areas of our conscious mentality are incidental and subordinate to those broad areas of which even the brightest minds of our race have merely explored the borderland; the expanded uncharted interior of the strange country still awaiting the exploring expeditions of the future. Our position in relation to this great *Terra Incognita* of the mind is similar to that of the ancient civilized world toward the earth as a whole; we are as yet awaiting the Columbus who will explore the Western Continent of the mind, and the Livingstones and Stanleys who will furnish us with maps of the mental Darkest Africa.

Yet, even the comparatively small explored areas of the Subconscious have revealed to us a wonderful land—a land filled with the richest raw materials, precious metals, wonderful species of animal and plant life. And our daring investigators have discovered means of applying and using some of the wonderful things which have been discovered in even that borderland of the new mental world.

The Subconscious entertains deep-rooted convictions and beliefs concerning the general success or non-success of the individual. The person who has constantly impressed upon his subconscious mentality that he is "unlucky" and that "Fate is against me," has created a tremendous power within himself which acts as a brake or obstacle to his successful achievement. He has created an enemy within himself which serves to hold him back, and which fights against every inner effort in the direction of success. This hidden enemy hampers his full efforts and cripples his activities.

On the contrary, the person who believes that "luck is running my way," and that "things are working in my favor," not only releases all of his latent energies but also actually stimulates his full powers—along subconscious lines as well as conscious.

Many men have become so convinced of their propitious Destiny that they have overcome obstacles which would have blocked the progress of one holding the opposite conviction. In fact, most of the men who have used their failures as stepping-stones to subsequent success have felt within themselves the conviction that they would triumph in the end, and that the disappointments and temporary failures were but incidents of the game.

Men have believed in their "stars" or in the presence and power of something outside of themselves which was operating in the direction of their ultimate triumph. This has given to them an indomitable will and an unconquerable spirit. Had these same men allowed the conviction of the operation of adverse and antagonistic influences to take possession of their souls, they would have gone down in the struggle—and would have stayed down. In either case, however, the real "something" which they have believed to be an outside thing or entity, has been nothing more nor less than the influence and power of their own Subconscious— in one case pulling with them, and in the other pulling against them.

The man with his Subconscious filled with belief and Faith in his non-success, and in the inevitable failure of his efforts—the man whose Confident Expectation is that of non-success, failure and inability, and whose Expectant Attention is directed toward such an outcome and the incidents and circumstances leading up to it,—is like a man in the water who is swimming against the stream. He is opposing the strong current, and his every effort is counteracted and overcome by the adverse forces of the stream. Likewise, the man whose Subconscious is saturated with the conviction of ultimate victory and final success—whose Confident Expectation is directed toward that end, and whose Expectant Attention is ever on the look-out for things tending to realize his inner beliefs—is like the swimmer who is moving in the direction of the current. Such a man not only is not really opposed by the forces of the stream, but, instead, has these forces at work aiding him.

The importance of having the Faith, Confident Expectation and Expectant Attention of the Subconscious directed toward your success, achievement and successful ultimate accomplishment—and the importance of not having these mighty forces operate against yourself—may be realized when you stop to consider that in the one case you have three-quarters of your mental equipment and power operating in your favor, and in the other case you have that three-quarters operating against you. And that three-quarters, in either case, not only is working actively during your waking hours, but also "works while you sleep." To lose the assistance of that three-quarters would be a serious matter would it not? But far more serious is it to have that three-quarters actually working against you—having it on the side of the enemy! This is just what happens when the Subconscious gets into action under the influence of wrongly directed Faith, Expectant Attention and Confident Expectation.

Get busy with your Subconscious. Train it, educate it, reeducate it, direct it, incline it, teach it, suggest to it, along the lines of the Faith in Success and Power and not those of the Faith in failure and weakness. Set it to work swimming with that current. The Subconscious is much given to Faith—it lives on Faith, it acts upon Faith. Then see that you supply it with the right kind of Faith, and avoid as a pestilence that Faith which is based on fear and is grounded in failure and despair. Think carefully—and act!

HOW TO DEVELOP ENTHUSIASM FOR YOUR WORK

Faith is the underlying principle of that remarkable quality of the human mind which is known as Enthusiasm. It is its essence, it is its substance, it is its actuating principle. Without Faith there can be no manifestation of Enthusiasm. Without Faith there can be no expression of the activities of Enthusiasm. Without Faith there can be no exhibition of the energies of Enthusiasm. Without Faith the quality of Enthusiasm remains dormant, latent and static—Faith is needed to arouse it, to render it active, to cause it to become dynamic.

Moreover, the Faith required for the manifestation and expression of Enthusiasm must be positive Faith—Faith in the successful outcome of the undertaking—Faith exhibiting its positive phases—Faith in the attainment of that which is desirable and which is regarded as good. You can never manifest Enthusiasm toward that which you confidently expect to be a failure, nor toward that which you feel will bring undesirable results and effects. Negative Faith has no power to arouse Enthusiasm; the presence of Positive Faith is necessary to awaken this wonderful latent mental or spiritual force.

Enthusiasm is a mental or spiritual force which has always been regarded by mankind with respect—often with a respect mingled with awe. To the ancients it seemed to be a special gift of the gods, and by them it was regarded as animating the individual with almost divine attributes of power, and as causing him to absorb a portion of the essence of the divine nature. Recognizing the fact that men under the influence of Enthusiasm often accomplish almost superhuman tasks, the ancients came to believe that this added power and capacity arose from the superimposition of power from planes of being above that of humanity. Hence, they employed terms to define it which clearly indicated their belief in its transcendent nature.

The term "Enthusiasm," is directly derived from the ancient Greek term meaning, "to be inspired by the gods." The two compositive elements of the original term are, respectively, a term denoting "inspiration," and one denoting "the gods" or "divinity," the two terms in combination meaning literally "inspired by the gods."

You have found that when you become quite intensely interested in a subject, object, study, pursuit or cause, so that your Enthusiasm is thoroughly aroused then there comes to you a highly increased and greatly intensified degree and amount of mental energy and power. At such times your mind seems to work with lightning-like rapidity, and with a wonderful sense of ease and efficiency. Your mental powers seem to be quadrupled—your mental machinery seems to have some miraculous oil poured into the proper place, thus removing all friction and allowing every part of the mechanism to move smoothly and easily and with wonderful speed. At such times you feel, indeed, actually "inspired." You feel that a new world of attainment would be opened to you if you could make this mental condition a permanent one.

Looking around you in your world of practical everyday work and effort, you will see why business men and other men of affairs regard as an important factor of successful work that mental quality known as "enthusiastic interest" on the part of the persons performing that work. This "enthusiastic interest" in the work or task is found to call forth all the mental and physical powers of the worker. He not only puts into his task every ounce of his ordinary capacity, but he also draws upon that hidden reserve force of his Subconscious mentality and adds that to his ordinary full energy. When he approaches the fatigue limit his "enthusiastic interest" carries him on, and before long he has "caught his second wind" and obtained his fresh start.

Ask any successful sales-manager for a list of the essential characteristics of the successful salesman, and on that list you will find this capacity for or habit of "enthusiastic interest" occupying a prominent place. This, not only because of its highly important effect upon the work of the salesman himself, but also because "Enthusiasm is contagious," and the lively, quickened interest of the salesman tends to communicate itself to the subconscious mentality of his customer.

In the same way the Enthusiasm of the public speaker, orator, advocate or statesman energizes and quickens his entire intellectual and emotional nature, thus causing him to do his best, likewise communicating itself to his audience by means of "mental contagion." The man with "his soul afire" tends to fire the souls and hearts of those around him. The spirit of the enthusiastic leader, foreman, or "boss" is "caught" by those under him.

Enthusiasm is clearly a manifestation of the emotional phase of man's mentality, and it appeals directly and immediately to the emotional nature of others. Likewise, it is clearly a product of the subconscious mentality, and accordingly it appeals directly and immediately to the subconscious mentality of others. Its effect is characteristically animating, energizing, inspiring, "quickening." It not only stirs the feelings and sets fire to the spiritual nature but it also stimulates and vivifies the intellectual faculties. The "live wires" in the world of men are those individuals who possess the quality of "enthusiastic interest" highly developed and habitually manifested when the occasion calls for it. Overdone, it defeats its object—the Golden Mean must be observed; but lacking it the man is what is known in the idiom of practical men as a "dead one."

The man of true Enthusiasm is characterized by his abiding Faith in his proposition or subject; by his lively interest in it; by his earnestness in presenting it and working toward its accomplishment; by his untiring, indefatigable efforts on its behalf. Faith, however, is the foundation upon which all the rest is built; lacking Faith, the structure of Enthusiasm falls like a house of cards.

The more Faith a man has in that which he is doing, toward which he is working, or that which he is presenting to others, the greater will be the manifestation of his own powers and capacity, the more efficient will be his performance of the work, and the greater will be his ability to influence others and to cause them to see things in the light of his own belief and interest. Faith arouses and sustains Enthusiasm; lack of

Faith deadens and inhibits it; Unfaith and positive disbelief kill it. It is clear that the first step toward the cultivation and development of Enthusiasm is that of the creation of Faith in the subject or object toward which you wish to manifest and express Enthusiasm.

If you have no Faith in the subject or object of your activities, then you will never be able to manifest Enthusiasm concerning that subject or object.

Life without Faith and Enthusiasm is a living death— persons living that life are mere walking corpses. If you would be a "live wire" instead of a "dead one," you must begin to arouse and develop Enthusiasm in your heart and soul. You must cultivate that keen and quickened Interest, and that lively and earnest Faith in what you are doing, and in the things to which you are giving your time and work. You must mentally "breathe in," and inspire that Spirit of Life which men for many centuries have called "Enthusiasm," and which is the twin-sister of Inspiration. Then will you know the exhilaration of that "enkindled and kindling fervor of soul"—that "ardent and lively zeal"— the mark of true Enthusiasm.

THE FLAME OF DESIRE ESSENTIAL TO FAITH

Desire is the second factor of Mental Power. You must not only "know definitely exactly what you want," and manifest it by means of Idealization; you must also "want it hard enough," and manifest it in Insistent Desire. Desire is the flame and fire which create the steam of Will. The Will never goes out into effective action except when drawn forth by active and sufficiently strong Desire. Desire furnishes the "motive" for Will; Will never becomes active in absence of a "motive." When we speak of a man having a "strong will," we often mean really that he has strong desire—Desire strong enough to cause him to exert every ounce of power and energy in him toward the attainment or accomplishment of the object of Desire.

Desire exerts a tremendous influence upon all of the mental faculties, causing them to put forth their full energies and powers and to perform their work efficiently. It stimulates the intellect, inspires the emotions and quickens the imagination. Without the urge of Desire there would be but little mental work performed. The keynote of Desire is "I Want"; and to gratify and satisfy that "want" the mind puts forth its best energies. Without Desire you would do but little thinking, for there would be no motive for such. Without Desire you would perform no actions, for there would be no moving-reason for such. Desire is ever the "mover to action"—to action mental as well as physical.

Moreover, the degree and the intensity of your work, mental or physical, is determined by the degree of Desire manifested in you concerning the object or end of such work. The more you want a thing, the harder will you work for it, and the easier will such work seem to you to be. The task performed under the influence and incentive of strong Desire will seem much easier than would be the same task performed without such influence and incentive—and infinitely easier than would the same task appear if its end and object were contrary to your Desire. No argument is needed to establish these facts—they are matters of common knowledge and are proved by the experience of everyday life.

The degree of force, energy, will, determination, persistence and continuous application manifested by an individual in his aspirations, ambitions, aims, performances, actions and work, is determined primarily by the degree of his Desire for the attainment of these objects—his degree of "want" and "want to" concerning that object. So true is this principle that some who have studied its effects have announced the aphorism: "You can have or be anything you want—if you only want it hard enough."

Without Faith it is practically impossible for you to manifest strong, ardent, insistent Desire. If you are filled with doubt, distrust, unfaith or disbelief in a thing, or concerning the successful accomplishment or attainment of anything, you will not be able to arouse the proper degree of desire for that thing or for its accomplishment and attainment. Lack of Faith, or, still more, positive disbelief, tends to paralyze the Desire Power; it acts as a brake or as a damper upon its power. Faith, on the contrary, frees the brakes of Desire, or turns on the full draft of its fire.

Here is the principle in concise form: Faith encourages and sustains, promotes and maintains Desire in its highest degree of efficiency; doubt, disbelief, distrust, and unfaith retard and restrict, inhibit and paralyze this efficient manifestation of Desire.

THE MIGHTY POWER OF A STRONG WILL

Will-Action is the third factor of Mental Power. You must not only "know clearly just what you 'want," and see it in your "mind's eye" in ideal form—you must not only "want it hard enough," and arouse its power to a degree of insistence and demand which will not brook denial or defeat—you must also call into service the persistent, determined, indomitable application of the Will, which will hold your energies and powers steadfastly and relentlessly to the task of accomplishment and attainment. You must "will to will" and must make your Will will itself in the act of Willing.

Will is perhaps the most mysterious of all of the mental powers. It seems to dwell on a mental plane alone by itself. It lies nearer and closer to the "I AM I" or Ego, than does any other phase of mentality. It is the principal instrument of the "I AM I"—the instrument which the latter employs directly and immediately. Its spirit is Persistent Determination—its essence is Action. Whenever you act, then do you employ your Will. Will Power is the dynamic phase or aspect of Mental Power. All other mental force is more or less static—it is only when the Will becomes involved in the process that Mental Power manifests its dynamic phase or aspect. Wise men have held that "All Power is Will Power at the last"; and that, "All activities are forms or phases of Will-Action, at the last." In the Cosmos, as well as in the individual, Will Power is the essential and basic phase of Power.

HOW TO ATTRACT THE PERSON YOU WANT

The Law of Mental Attraction, or Mental Gravitation, acts along lines very similar to those of the action of physical Gravitation. There is present and active the mutual and reciprocal "pull" between Thoughts and Things, and between Thoughts and Thoughts—Thoughts, however, are Things at the last analysis. This principle extends even to so-called inanimate objects: this mystery is explainable under the now well-established law that there is Mind in everything, even in the apparently inanimate objects of the universe, even in the atoms and particles of which material substances are composed.

Not only do you attract thought-vibrations, thought-waves, thought-currents, thought-atmospheres, etc. of a harmonious character, and to which your thoughts have a natural affinity; you also attract to yourselves (by the power of thought attraction) other persons whose thoughts have an affinity and harmony with your own. In the same way you attract to yourself (and are attracted toward) other persons whose interests run along the same general lines as your own.

You draw to yourself the persons who may be necessary for the successful carrying out of the plans and purposes, the desires and ambitions, which fill your thoughts most of the time; and, in the same way, you are drawn toward those into whose plans and purposes you are fitted to play an important part. In short, each person tends to attract toward himself those other persons whom he needs in order to materialize his ideals and to express his desires— providing that he "wants hard enough" and providing that the other persons are in harmonious affinity with his plans and purposes.

Persons who have had their attention directed toward the operations of the Law of Mental Attraction, and who have learned to apply the principles of its manifestation in their own affairs in life, observe many wonderful instances of its power in the happenings of their everyday life. Books, newspaper items, magazine articles bearing on some subject which is prominent in their thoughts, all these come to hand in an almost uncanny way. Persons who fit into the general scheme of the thought-plan come into one's life. Peculiar "happenings" come to pass in the same way. Things arise which "fit in" with the general idea. Unexpected circumstances arise which, although often at first sight seemingly obstructive and undesirable, in the end are found to dovetail perfectly into the whole scheme of things. No wonder that many persons having these experiences are at first inclined to attribute them to supernatural or superhuman influence—but they are in full accordance with Natural Law, and are a part of the powers of man, when rightly understood.

Your conditions and environment, the circumstances and happenings which come to you, are very largely the result of the operation of the Law of Mental Attraction—and they are accordingly, to a great extent, manifestations in objective, material form of your mental ideas, ideals and pictures, the force and nature of such manifestation depending largely upon the degree of Faith and Confident Expectation possessed and expressed by you in your thoughts upon these subjects and events—or upon the degree of doubt, disbelief, distrust and unfaith, those negative phases of Faith which serve to slow down the action of Faith Power or perhaps even to reverse its machinery.

You create environment, conditions, circumstances, events, assistance, means to ends, by Mental Power operating along the lines of the Law of Mental Attraction. Mental Attraction, like all forms or phases of Mental Power, is the transformation of the subjective Ideal into objective Reality—the thought tends to take form in action, the mental form tends to take on objective materiality and substance. The ideal is represented by the clear, strong, definite, mental picture or ideal form manifested in Idealization. Desire furnishes the flame and heat which generate the steam of Will needed in the creative process; but the Idealization is impaired and weakened, the Desire dies away, the Will loses its determination, unless Faith be there to create the Confident Expectation. The less the Faith and Confident Expectation, or the greater the doubt, disbelief, distrust, unfaith and lack of confidence, the weaker is the Idealization, the weaker the Desire, and the weaker the Will Power manifested.

Without Faith there can be no Confident Expectation; without Faith, the Fires of Desire die away; without Faith, the Steam of Will ceases to be generated; and thus Attainment becomes impossible. Whenever you think of the Law of Mental Attraction, think of Faith—for Faith is its very soul—its inspiration.

BELIEVE IN YOURSELF

Among the many characteristics and qualities which make for success of the individual there is none more fundamental, essential and basic than that of Self Confidence and Self Reliance—both of these terms being but expressions of the idea of Faith in Oneself. The man who has Faith in himself not only brings under his control and direction those wonderful powers of his subconscious mentality, and the full power of his conscious mental faculties and instruments, but also tends to inspire a similar feeling in the minds and hearts of those other individuals with whom he comes in contact in the course of his pursuit of the objects of his endeavors. An intuitive perception and realization of one's own powers and energies, capacity, and efficiency, possibilities and capabilities, is an essential attribute of the individual who is destined to success.

A study of the world of men will disclose the fact that those men who eventually succeed, who "arrive" ultimately, who "do things," are marked by this deep intuitive Faith in themselves, and by their Confident Expectation of Ultimate success. These men rise superior to the incidents of temporary defeat; they use these failures as stepping-stones to ultimate victory. They are living expressions of Henley's *Invictus*—they, indeed, are the Masters of their Fate, the Captains of their Souls! Such men are never Really defeated; like rubber balls, they have that "bounce" which causes them to rise Triumphantly after each fall—the harder they are "thrown down," the higher do they rise on the rebound. Such men are always possible—nay, probable and certain—victors, so long as they maintain this intuitive Faith in Self, of Self Confidence; it is only when this is lost that they are really defeated or destroyed.

The failures in life are discovered usually to be either (1) those who have never manifested this Faith in Self, or Self Confidence; or else (2) those who have permitted themselves to lose the same under the "Bludgeonings of Chance."

Those who have never felt the thrill of Faith in Self, or of Self Confidence, are soon labeled by their fellows as lacking the elements of successful achievement—the world soon "gets their number" and places them where they belong. Their lack of Self Faith and Self Confidence is felt by those with whom they come in contact; the world lacks Faith in them and has no Confident Expectation of their success.

The study of the life-story of the successful men in all walks of life will illustrate this principle to you so forcibly that, having perceived it, you will never again doubt its absolute truth. In practically every case you will find that these successful men have been knocked down, and bowled out, many times in the early days of their careers—often even later on in life. But the knock-out, though perhaps dazing them for a short time, never robbed them of their gameness, their will-to-succeed. They always arose to their feet before they were counted out; and they always firmly, but resolutely, faced Fate. Though their "heads were bloody, they were unbowed," as Henley triumphantly chants. Fate cannot defeat such a spirit; in time, Destiny recognizes the fact that "here is a man"—and being feminine, she falls in love with him and bestows her favors upon him.

When you have found your Real Self—"That Something Within"—this "I AM I"—then have you found that Inner and Real Self which has constituted the subject and object of that Faith and Confident Expectation which have inspired, animated, enthused and sustained the thousands of men who have reached the Heights of Attainment by the Path of Definite Ideals, Insistent Desire, Confident Expectation, Persistent Determination, and Balanced Compensation. It is this Intuitive perception and consciousness of the Real Self which has caused men to live out the ideal of *Invictus* in the spirit of that glorious poem of Henley. Nothing but this inner realization would have been sufficient to fill the soul of man with this indomitable spirit and unconquerable will.

INVICTUS
BY W. E. HENLEY

Out of the night that covers me,
* Black as the pit from pole to pole,*
I thank whatever gods there be
* For my unconquerable soul.*

In the fell clutch of circumstance
* I have not winced or cried aloud;*

Under the bludgeonings of chance
   My head is bloody but unbowed.

Beyond this vale of doubt and fear
   Looms but the terror of the Shade
And, yet, the passing of the years
   Finds, and shall find me, unafraid.

It matters not how straight the gate,
   How charged with punishments the scroll
I am the Master of my Fate,
   I am the Captain of my Soul.

The wise teachers of the race have for centuries taught that this Faith in the Real Self, in the "I AM I," will enable the individual to convert into the instruments of his success even those circumstances which apparently are destined to defeat his purposes; and to transmute into beneficent agencies even those inimical forces which beset him on all sides. They have discovered, and passed on to their followers, the knowledge, that such a Faith is a spiritual Power, a living force, which when trusted and rightly employed will annihilate the opposition of outward circumstances, or else convert them into workers for good.

Your Real Self is a ray from the great Sun of Spirit—a spark from the great Flame of Spirit—a focal point of expression of that infinite SELF OF SPIRIT.

The earnest Faith in your Real Self, and your Confident Expectation concerning its manifestation and expression in your work, your endeavors, your plans, your purposes, serve to bring into action your full mental and spiritual power, energy, and force. It quickens your intellectual powers; it employs your emotional powers efficiently and under full control; it sets into effective action your creative imagination; it places the powers of your will under your mastery and direction. It draws upon your subconscious faculties for inspiration and for intuitive reports; it opens up your mind to the inflow of the illumination of your superconscious spiritual faculties and powers. It sets into operation the

Law of Mental Attraction under your direct control and direction, whereby you attract to yourself, or you to them, the circumstances, events, conditions, things and persons needed for the manifestation of your ideals in objective reality. More than this, it brushes away the obstacles which have clogged the channels of your contact with and communication with SPIRIT itself—that great source of Infinite Power which in this instruction is called POWER.

Discover your Real Self, your "I AM I"—then manifest your full Faith in and toward it; and cultivate your full Confident Expectation concerning the beneficent results of that Faith.

THE INFINITE LOVES YOU
BECOME AN INVINCIBLE SOUL

The Message of Truth: You, yourself, in your essential and real being, nature, and entity, are Spirit, and naught but Spirit—in and of SPIRIT; spiritual and not material. Materiality is your instrument of expression, the stuff created for your use and service in your expression of Life, Consciousness and Will: it is your servant, not your master; you condition, limit and form it, not it you, when you recognize and realize your real nature, and awaken to a perception of its real relation to you and you to it. The report of SPIRIT received by its accredited individual centers of expression, and by them transmitted to you is this:

In the degree that you perceive, recognize, and realize your essential identity with ME, the Supreme Presence-Power, the Ultimate Reality, in that degree will you be able to manifest My Spiritual Power. I AM over and above you, under and beneath you, I surround you on all sides. I AM also within you, and you are in ME; from Me you proceed and in Me you live and move and have your being. Seek Me by looking within your own being, and likewise by looking for Me in Infinity, for I abide both within and without your being. If, and when, you will adopt and live according to this Truth, then will you be able to manifest that Truth—in and by it alone are Freedom and Invincibility, and true and real Presence and Power, to be found, perceived, realized and manifested.

Francis Thompson, in his mystic poem entitled *The Hound of Heaven* describes with a tremendous power, and often with an almost terrible intensity, the hunt of Reality for the unwilling individual Self. He pictures Divinity as engaged in a remorseless, tireless quest—a seeking, following, tracking-down of the unwilling individual soul. He pictures the separated spirit as a "strange, piteous, futile thing" that flees from the pursuing Divinity "down the nights and down the days." The individual spirit, not knowing its relation to and identity with the pursuing Absolute, rushes in a panic of terror away from its own good. But, as Emerson says, "You cannot escape your own Good"; and, so the fleeing soul is captured at last. By Faith in the Infinite, however, the individual soul overcomes its terror of the Infinite and, recognizing it as its Supreme Good, it turns and moves toward it. Such is the mystic conception of the effect and action of Faith in the Infinite.

The complete poem, *The Hound of Heaven*, covers five pages; but we here present a condensed version of these beautiful and gripping lines by Francis Thompson. If you are not reciprocating the Great Love of God, you may have a feeling of remorse and resolve to do better. If this feel: does not come to you; you must have a heart of stone.

THE HOUND OF HEAVEN
BY FRANCIS THOMPSON

I fled Him, down the nights and down the days;
   I fled Him, down the arches of the years;
I fled Him, down the labyrinthine ways
   Of my own mind; and in the mist of tears
I hid from Him, and under running laughter.
   Up vistaed hopes I sped;
   And shot, precipitated,
Adown Titanic glooms of chasmed fears,
From those strong Feet that followed, followed after.
   But with unhurrying chase,
   And unperturbed pace,
Deliberate speed, majestic instancy,
   They beat—and a Voice beat
   More instant that the Feet—
"All things betray thee, who betrayest Me."

I said to Dawn: Be sudden—to Eve: Be soon;
   With thy young skiey blossoms heap me over
   From this tremendous Lover—

Still with unhurrying chase,
And unperturbed pace,
Deliberate speed, majestic instancy,
   Came on the following Feet,

And a voice above their beat—
"Naught shelters thee, who wilt not shelter Me."

In the rash lustihead of my young powers,
   I shook the pillaring hours
And pulled my life upon me; grimed with smears,
I stand amid the dust of the mounded years—
My mangled youth lies dead beneath the heap.
 My days have crackled and gone up in smoke.
   Designer Infinite!—
Ah! must Thou char the wood ere Thou canst limn with it?
My freshness spent its wavering shower in the dust;
And now my heart is as a broken fount.

   Now of that long pursuit
   Comes on at hand the bruit;
  That Voice is round me like a bursting sea:
"How little worthy of any love thou art!
Whom wilt thou find to love ignoble thee
   Save Me, save only Me?
All which I took from thee I did but take,
   Not for thy harms,
But just that thou mightest seek it in My arms.
   All which thy child's mistake
Fancies as lost, I have stored for thee at home:
   Rise, clasp My hand, and come!"

   Halts by me that footfall:
   Is my gloom, after all,
Shade of His hand, outstretched caressingly?
   "Ah, fondest, blindest, weakest,
   I am He Whom thou seekest!
Thou dravest love from thee, who dravest Me."

Prentice Mulford said: "A Supreme Power and Wisdom governs the Universe. The Supreme Mind is measureless and pervades all space. The Supreme Wisdom, Power, and Intelligence are in everything that exists, from the atom to the planet. The Supreme Power has us in its charge, as it has the suns and endless system of worlds in space. As we grow more to recognize this sublime and exhaustless Wisdom, we shall learn more and more to demand that Wisdom, draw it to ourselves, and thereby be ever making ourselves newer and newer. This means ever perfecting health, greater power to enjoy all that exists, gradual transition into a higher state of being, and the development of powers which we do not now realize as belonging to us. Let us then daily demand Faith, for Faith is power to believe and power to see that all things are parts of the Infinite Spirit of God, that all things have Good or God in them, and that all things, when recognized by us as parts of God, must work for our good."

To sum up:

1. There exists a greater underlying Something that is beneficent and well-disposed toward you, and which tries to help, aid and assist you whenever and wherever It can do so.

2. Faith and Confident Expectation regarding the beneficent power of that Something tends to open the channels of Its influence in your life; while doubt, unbelief, distrust, and fear, tend to dam up the channel of its influence in your life, and to rob it of the power to help you.

3. To a great extent, at least, you determine your own life by the character of your thought; by the nature and character of your thoughts you furnish the pattern or mold which determines or modifies the efforts of the Something to aid you, either in the direction of producing desirable results or else in bringing about undesirable results by reason of your damming up the sources of your Good.

In the *Book of Psalms* in our own Scriptures, are to be found several of the great masterpieces of the esoteric teachings concerning Faith Power—in them is given the essence of the Secret Doctrine concerning Faith in the Infinite. Chief among these are the Twenty-Third Psalm, and the Ninety-first Psalm, respectively. So important are these two great esoteric poems—so filled with practical helpful information are they—that we deem it advisable to reproduce them here that you may avail yourself of their virtue and power at this particular stage of this instruction. Accordingly, they are given on these pages.

THE PSALM OF FAITH
Psalm 23

The Lord is my shepherd; I shall not want. He maketh me to lie down in the green pastures; he leadeth me beside the still waters. He restoreth my soul; he leadeth me in the paths of righteousnes for His name's sake. Yea, though I walk through the valley of the shadow of death, I will fear no evil; for thou art with me; Thy rod and Thy staff they comfort me. Thou preparest a table before me in the presence of mine enemies; Thou anointest my head with oil; my cup runneth over. Surely goodness and mercy will follow me all the days of my life, and I will dwell in the house of the Lord forever.

THE PSALM OF SECURITY
Psalm 91

He that dwelleth in the secret place of the most High shall abide under the shadow of the Almighty. I will say of the Lord, He is my refuge and my fortress: my God in Him will I trust. Surely He shall deliver thee from the snare of the fowler, and from the noisome pestilence. He shall cover thee with His feathers, and under His wings shalt thou trust: His truth shall be thy shield and buckler. Thou shalt not be afraid for the terror by night; nor for the arrow that flieth by day; nor for the pestilence that walketh in darkness; nor for the destruction that wasteth at noonday. A thousand shall fall at thy side, and ten thousand at thy right hand; but it shall not come nigh thee. Only with thine eyes shalt thou behold and see the reward of the wicked. Because thou hast made the Lord, which is my refuge, even the most high, thy habitation. There shall no evil befall thee, neither shall any plague come nigh thy dwelling. For He shall give His angels charge over thee, to keep thee in all thy ways. They shall bear thee up in their hands, lest thou dash thy foot against a stone. Thou shalt tread upon the lion and the adder: the young lion and the dragon shalt thou trample under feet. Because he hath set his love upon Me, and therefore will I deliver him; I will set him on high, because he hath known My name. He shall call upon Me, and I will answer him and honor him. With long life will I satisfy him, and show him my salvation.

LEAD KINDLY LIGHT

The teachers and students of the Inner teachings, the Ancient Wisdom, the Secret Doctrine, are also aware of the esoteric

spiritual significance of the lines of the well-known hymn "Lead Kindly Light," written by Newman in a period of spiritual stress. Few who read or sing this hymn realize its esoteric spirit and meaning—none but "those who know" perceive and recognize that which dwells under the surface of those wonderful words and lines.

THE CHANT OF FAITH POWER
(Lead Kindly Light)
Lead kindly Light, amid the encircling gloom; Lead Thou
me on. The night is dark, and I am far from home; Lead
Thou
me on. Keep Thou my feet; I do not ask to see the distant
scene;
one step enough for me, Lead Thou me on.

Carry with you ever the spirit of the ancient aphorism of the wise sage, which is; "Faith is the White Magic of Power."

Bigger not so great

12 mo Onesie

S 2-4   Toddler
M -10-12   Best
L 14-16   2 3 4 all the same   Add a Kid

3 or 4
per size

Lowell + Don
owners

(TOM Bohinsky)

Very specific
name drop. Re
6 different
designs

400 designs

justaddakid.com

free sample   product index
+ Style

MIX BIBS
MIX SIZES
12/Styles des 15"
72 pieces

(24 pieces)
min.

d Surely much
larger

any combo   Name Drop
(Dana)   Biggest

6 per design -
(But Can do Smaller)

$20 transports

1800 H
Ivy

hotel/airport   Artists
hospitals   do name drop
museum
casino's   not Hallmark

144 piece
to Gatlinburg

$21 - fits in
24 × 12 × 18"

no wood
displays

3 poles

counter
48 piece

Large
~~$~~

144 piece
display

$60

some should
be Backstock

6.75
disp 50

3.5" 99%
of IV poles

disposable

displays
IV pole
$1\frac{1}{2} \times 1\frac{1}{2} - 2.3$
spenser
rack

Derek
5/14
457-
6493

6⁹⁹ - 9⁹⁹
3⁴⁹ - 4⁹⁹
wholesale
min. 200/shop
3 dozen - 4 doz.
w/ display
ca pick or prepare

CPSIA information can be obtained at www.ICGtesting.com
Printed in the USA
268993BV00001B/10/P